MORE SPARKS FROM ZION

DAVID RUBIN

Shiloh
ISRAELPress

More Sparks From Zion
ISBN 978-0-9829067-8-1

Published by Shiloh Israel Press

www.ShilohIsraelChildren.org
www.DavidRubinIsrael.com
www.Facebook.com/DavidRubin.Shiloh.Israel

Contact The Author
David@ShilohIsraelChildren.org
1-845-738-1522

Contact The Publisher
sipress@ShilohIsraelChildren.org

For Orders
1-800-431-1579 (toll-free)

Book Development and Production
Chaim Mazo – chaim.mazo@gmail.com

Cover Design and Layout
Christopher Tobias

Printed in Israel

This book is dedicated to the victims of the daily terror attacks in Israel, as well as those in Belgium, France, the United States, and other parts of the free world. All were brutally murdered or wounded for being in the path of the increasingly emboldened Islamic tsunami.

Contents

Introduction

ISIS ... Hamas ... Islamic Jihad ... Hezbollah ... Al Qaeda ... Fatah ... Boko Haram ... Taliban – What do all of these terrorist organizations have in common? They all possess a rabid hatred of Israel, along with a fierce animosity towards Judeo-Christian civilization. Furthermore, they all support and carry out armed attacks against civilians in Israel and the West.

While confronting these serious security threats, Israel faces internal threats from a political polarization and complicated secular-religious divisions that could also imperil the nation's ability to move forward with resolve.

In the past couple of years, we have witnessed political turmoil in Israel, as voters went to the polls at the end of a raucous electoral season. At the height of the campaign, Muslim terrorists created havoc with a string of terror attacks in France, momentarily reminding the world once again that Israel's ongoing challenge of combatting radical Islam is not its own. Could it be that the rest of the free world is in danger, as well?

The recent multiple attacks in Paris and Brussels shocked the world in their intensity and ruthlessness, as did the beheadings in London, Iraq, and elsewhere. The images of young, male Muslim immigrants flooding into Europe under the dubious claim of refugee status has disturbed citizens of the free nations, as the correlating rapes and harassment of European women are skyrocketing. Politicians have seemed almost at a loss to explain the cause of the terrorism or even to identify the real enemy. They have been stuttering and stumbling over their words, while trying to suggest real solutions. Even the fiery Republican candidate for president of the United States, Donald Trump, while boldly suggesting a ban on Muslim immigration, quickly qualified his proposal, stating that it would be temporary, "until we figure out what's going on."

Nonetheless, some world leaders, including the one that inhabited the White House from 2009-2016, failed to recognize, or at least refused to acknowledge the Islamic threat to world peace and freedom. Trump was targeted by political figures as diverse as Democratic presidential candidate Hillary Clinton, by GOP House Speaker Paul Ryan, and by Sadiq Khan, the new Muslim Mayor of London, for his comments calling for a temporary ban on Muslim immigration to the United States. This sharp criticism of Trump could be considered reasonable in normal times, but coming as it does, in the shadow of the mass immigration of Muslims to Europe that is profoundly changing the very face of the old continent, the criticism rings hollow, as it represents a sad state of confusion.

So where does all of this madness leave Israel, that tiny reestablished country perpetually surrounded by Islamic fundamentalism? Barely the size of the American state of New Jersey, Israel faces multiple growing threats, not only terrorism at home, but also an increasing nuclear threat from the ayatollahs of Iran, with whom the Obama administration recently signed a nuclear deal.

> "For thus says the Lord of hosts – After His glory has He sent me unto the nations which plundered you: for he that touches you touches the apple of His eye."
>
> *(Zechariah 2:8)*

Israel is a microcosm of the greater Islamic threat to Judeo-Christian civilization, and therefore, all eyes will be on Israel as the global challenge increases. But it's actually much bigger than that, for Israel has always been the center of the world's attention.

> "I will also make you a light unto the nations, that
> My salvation may reach to the ends of the earth."
>
> *(Isaiah 49:6)*

Yes, Israel is the biblical nation, the nation that was chosen for a higher purpose. It is in this context that one can begin to understand why Israel is always at the center of the news. In this context of Israel as the example to the world, one can fully understand the critical importance of how Israel relates to world events and, perhaps more significantly, how it relates to itself. Israel's internal politics are dynamic and fierce because there is an ongoing internal struggle over the character of the modern Israeli nation.

The basic questions over Israel's destiny go something like this: "Will Israel be a light unto the nations or simply a little, quirky nation among all the other nations? Will it be a religious or a secular nation?" and furthermore, "Will Israel take an assertive leadership role among the nations or will it be a subservient vassal state to its Western bosses?" That seeming dichotomy has ramifications for how Israel will confront all of the above critical issues.

For that reason, we will begin this book with Israel's combative internal politics and from there we'll address the critical international issues that the entire world is talking about. The articles in this collection, first published on Arutz Sheva (Israel National News), are the chronological follow-up to their predecessor, "Sparks From Zion", and they honestly confront the critical issues of the day that the "lamestream" media often avoids. Let's begin...

Israel's News Glossary

Politicians In The News

Abbas, Mahmoud – President of the Palestinian Authority, leader of the Fatah terrorist organization.

Bennett, Naftali – Israeli Economy Minister, leader of the Bayit Yehudi party, previously a self-made millionaire in the high-tech industry.

Bishara, Azmi – Former Knesset member, passionate Arab anti-Zionist accused of assisting Israel's enemies in wartime, among other treasonous crimes.

Diskin, Yuval – Former Israeli Intelligence official, who holds decidedly left-wing views on many issues of national security.

Erekat, Saeb – Palestinian Authority's lead negotiator.

Herzog, Yitzhak (Buji) – Leader of the Opposition (Left-Wing) Labor Party.

Hotovely, Tzipi – Member of Knesset from the right-wing of the centrist Likud party.

Kahlon, Moshe – Finance Minister, Leader of the Kulanu Party.

Lapid, Yair – Israeli Finance Minister, leader of the Yesh Atid party, formerly a popular talk show host, author, and journalist.

Liberman, Avigdor – Israeli Defense Minister (2016), leader of the Yisrael Beytenu party.

Livni, Tzipi – Israeli Minister of Justice, leader of the HaTnuah party, was in charge of peace negotiations with the Palestinian Authority.

Mashal, Khaled – Hamas terrorist organization leader.

Netanyahu, Benjamin (Binyamin) – Prime Minister of Israel, leader of the Likud political party.

Oren, Michael – Former Israeli Ambassador to the United States.

Peres, Shimon – Nonagenarian Israeli politician and former president; as Foreign Minister he was the primary architect of the Oslo Accords and has continued to be a passionate peace process advocate.

Rivlin, Reuven – President of Israel, long-time Likud politician and eighth-generation Israeli.

Smotrich, Bezalel – Freshman Member of Knesset, Jewish Home-Tekuma party.

Ya'alon, Moshe – Israeli Defense Minister – 2012-2016.

Terms In The News

Aliyah – The movement of the Jewish people returning to live in the Land of Israel.

Areas A, B, C – Division of authority in Judea and Samaria as defined in the Oslo Accords:
    Area A – Full Palestinian Authority autonomy.
    Area B – Palestinian Authority administrative authority, Israeli security authority.
    Area C – Full Israeli authority.

Fatah – The presumed "moderate" Islamic terrorist organization, which is the core of the Palestinian Authority, founded by Yasser Arafat and subsequently led by his successor, Mahmoud Abbas.

Hamas – The Islamic terrorist organization, which is rooted in the Muslim Brotherhood, and has been fighting against Israel from its base in Gaza, but not only.

Hezbollah – Shiite Islamic terrorist organization, based in Lebanon, part of the governing coalition and closely aligned with, and militarily supplied by Iran.

ISIS – The Islamic State in Syria and Iraq – the unabashedly ruthless Islamic terrorist organization; also known as ISIL or IS.

Jihad – Islamic holy war.

Levy Report – Officially known as the Report on the Legal Status of Building in Judea and Samaria, this 89-page report on the settlements was published on July 9, 2012, after extensive legal and historical research by a three-member committee headed by former Supreme Court Justice Edmund Levy. The report concluded that Israel's presence in Judea and Samaria (the West Bank) cannot accurately be called an occupation and that the Israeli communities in these areas are legal under international law.

MK – Minister of Knesset (Member of the Israeli Parliament).

Oslo Accords – "Peace" agreements secretly negotiated by Israel and the Palestine Liberation Organization and initialed in 1993, starting a process of Israeli withdrawal and/or disengagement from the regions of Judea, Samaria, and Gaza.

Palestinian Authority (PA) – Created by the Oslo Accords as the autonomous quasi-governmental authority in Area A and partially in Area B.

Price Tag Vandalism – Acts of vandalism, presumed by the media to have been carried out by Jews, although in most cases unproven, usually against Islamic or Arab mosques or other institutions, in revenge for terrorist attacks against Jews.

West Bank – the Arab-coined modern term for the contiguous regions of Samaria (north of Jerusalem) and Judea (south of Jerusalem), otherwise known as the historical biblical heartland of Israel.

Major Israeli Political Parties

Bayit Yehudi (Eng: Jewish Home) – a right-wing political party based on the principles of Religious Zionism, which recently united under the broad umbrella of Israelis who respect Jewish tradition and are faithful to the Land of Israel.

HaTnuah – A left-wing political party established by Tzipi Livni with the central purpose of furthering the peace process and preventing nationalistic initiatives.

Kadima – A formerly large, now small and insignificant political party originally started by former Prime Minister Ariel Sharon, Ehud Olmert, and Tzipi Livni for the purpose of carrying out the Israeli withdrawal from Gaza and the destruction of Israeli communities there in 2005.

Kulanu – First-term political party established by former Likud minister Moshe Kahlon to achieve power by attracting centrist votes.

Labor – A secular, left-wing political party, which for many years was the ruling party in Israel.

Likud – The leading political party in Israel, mostly secular, but considered to be right of center, and most recently led by Prime Minister Benjamin Netanyahu.

Shas – An ultra-Orthodox (Haredi) political party, established with the aim of restoring religious/ethnic pride to the large public of Sephardic Jews. Despite its religious ultra-Orthodox emphasis, it has taken many left of center positions on issues such as the peace process and social welfare.

Union of Arab parties – First-term political party established by the merging of several Arab parties into one unified party, thereby creating a more potent vehemently anti-Israel force in the Knesset.

UTJ (United Torah Judaism) – An ultra-Orthodox (Haredi) political party representing the public of Ashkenazi ultra-Orthodox Jews.

Yesh Atid (Eng: There is a Future) – A secular, left of center political party founded by former journalist Yair Lapid in 2012 that seeks to represent what it considers the center of Israeli society: the secular middle class.

Yisrael Beytenu (Eng: Israel Our Home) – A secular, right of center political party founded by Avigdor Liberman. The party's base has traditionally been Russian-speaking Israelis.

MORE SPARKS FROM ZION

*Who will rise up for me
against the evildoers?*

(Psalms 94:16)

When A Top Cop Plays Politician

"So much of left-wing thought is a kind of playing with fire by people who don't even know that fire is hot."

(George Orwell, British novelist, essayist, journalist and critic)

There are many people in a society who play the important role of being advocates for political viewpoints and the public debate of other controversial issues – politicians, opinion columnists, and legalists among them. However, there are other individuals who show a propensity to get into the fray, but don't belong there.

One such case in point is the current Police Commissioner Yohanan Danino, whose role as the leading police official is to oversee the proper enforcement of the law, not to be an advocate for a particular political viewpoint. Danino crossed that dangerous line, criticizing Attorney General Yehudah Weinstein for enabling right-wing politicians to "incite Arab unrest" by visiting the Temple Mount.

Showing a disturbing lack of professionalism, the top police official whined about an "extreme right-wing agenda to change the status quo on the Temple Mount," adding, "Anyone who wants to change the status quo on the Temple Mount should not be allowed up there."

Whether his position has any merit or not, and I don't believe it does, he is way out of line in turning his position of responsibility into a bully pulpit, at tax-payer expense, for his decidedly left-wing point of view. His job at this time is to enforce the status quo, which is the current government policy, but simultaneously, to respect the right to peaceful protest, freedom of movement, and freedom of speech, without letting his political biases get in the way. It's an admittedly difficult balancing act, but one that is incumbent on a public servant in his position.

Now as for that political viewpoint that was so inappropriately voiced by Danino, there is nothing "extreme" or "right-wing" about citizens or Knesset members calling for freedom of movement for all and for freedom of worship for all at Judaism's holiest site. The proposed changes, which would enable the peaceful exercise of those freedoms, need to be discussed in the appropriate forums by those who are elected by the people of Israel.

The place for that necessary debate is in Israel's legislature, the Knesset, not in the National Police Headquarters.

New Elections: Why Is it Happening – Where is it Going?

"A politician thinks of the next election. A statesman, of the next generation."

(James Freeman Clarke, American theologian and author)

After the latest clash between Prime Minister Netanyahu (Likud) and Finance Minister Yair Lapid (Yesh Atid), it has become clear that Israel is heading to early elections, with only half of the current term having been concluded. The main questions:

- Why couldn't this coalition last?

- What can we expect in the upcoming election campaign? In other words, who will be the winners/ losers and what will be the surprises?

Several things were working against the long-term cohesion of the current coalition from the start, although there was some short-term unity of purpose on particular issues.

There was unity, more or less, on the basics of promoting a free market economy, while encouraging employment to reduce poverty. That issue was one of the unifying factors that led to the draft law, which was designed, for all its flaws, to gradually move towards a more equal arrangement of military service and work in Israeli society, which, if successful, still has the potential to reduce poverty, strengthen the army, and bring the various sectors of society together.

There was also unity of purpose on the issue of making government smaller and decreasing the amount of parties.

This was accomplished by raising the minimum amount of votes needed by each party, a positive change which forces the members of the resultant larger parties to actually try to work together. The current tension between Uriel Ariel's Tekuma faction and Bayit Yehudi party leader Naftali Bennett is a case in point. The differences on issues of substance are relatively small and certainly don't warrant another national religious break-off party, which not only would hurt Bayit Yehudi's present and future growth, but would most likely leave Tekuma out of the Knesset since it would be unlikely to get the minimum number of votes, thereby ignoring the will of its voters. In short, under the current system, it is certainly worthwhile to resolve differences over the selection of candidates. A free and fair primary in Bayit Yehudi in which all party members can vote will result in a candidates list and a party platform that will reflect the will of the voters. Break-off parties no longer have a good chance of getting elected and for that reason, it pays to unite.

The problem with the current coalition was that with all of these challenges having been at least partially legislated, there were fewer unifying issues on the coalition agenda, which shifted the focus to the more ideological, hence more divisive issues, such as the Jewish State bill, relations with the Palestinian Authority's Hamas-Fatah government, or ending the unofficial freeze on the issuing of new permits for Jews to build homes in Judea, Samaria, and Jerusalem. While targeted cutting of taxes can often be very useful in a free economy, Finance Minister Yair Lapid's 0% VAT law was only necessary because of a simultaneous and irrational freeze on building in the biblical heartland of Israel. Opening up the markets would bring a boom in Judea, Samaria, and Jerusalem, which in turn would lower the cost of housing throughout the country. This was but one divisive issue that tore apart the coalition.

Last but not least, it is true that Ministers Yair Lapid (Yesh Atid) and Tzipi Livni (HaTnuah) seemed to often forget that they were a part of a coalition that didn't reflect their left-wing agenda. In fact, Lapid seemed to foolishly move further left as the months progressed and as his poll numbers dropped.

So what can we expect in these elections? Every election campaign has its own unexpected twists and turns, but some trends are clear:

1. The Likud should be able to hold its own, especially if it runs a clear issues-oriented campaign and avoids (unlike last time) bashing the national religious public and its rabbis, a foolish strategy that turned off more voters from voting Likud than from voting Bayit Yehudi.

2. Israel Beytenu will lose some of its strength, especially with party leader Avigdor Liberman's anticipated promotion of his "Divide the Land" peace plan, which will cost him some right-wing voters without bringing in the moderates.

3. Yesh Atid will lose at least several seats, partially due to the need for a finance minister to call for unpopular cutbacks in public services, but mostly due to the arrogant and often amateurish way that its leader and a few of his top associates related to coalition colleagues and to Prime Minister Netanyahu.

4. Bayit Yehudi will grow substantially if, and only if, unity, or at least the appearance of unity is achieved. National religious and traditional voters get very upset when there is an absence of peace in the Jewish home or, in this case, in the Jewish Home party (Bayit Yehudi).

5. Look for a slight rise in the UTJ numbers and a drop in mandates for Shas, which has been reduced in stature since the loss of its spiritual leader, Rabbi Ovadia Yosef.

6. The Arab parties will at least partially merge, thereby keeping their current strength.

7. Last but not least, former Likud Minister Moshe Kahlon's new party will become the latest, if not the greatest, "center party", the perennial "surprise" party that everyone will be talking about. This will be especially true if he places on his candidates list an interesting and diverse mix of name personalities who have so far avoided controversy. On the downside, these parties that try to attract non-ideological "stars" usually don't seem to last, or at least always lose popularity after the election. Just ask Yair Lapid and his 19-seat "centrist party" about that.

Making Peace In The Jewish Home

"We are only as strong as we are united, as weak as we are divided."

(J.K. Rowling, British novelist, screenwriter and film producer)

As Israel seems to be shifting into election mode, the Bayit Yehudi (Jewish Home) Party is continuing the infighting that has plagued the national religious public for many years and that we had thought was behind us. Once again, there is talk of a possible split between Bayit Yehudi under the leadership of Economy Minister Naftali Bennett and its ostensibly more right-wing and more religious Tekuma faction, headed by Housing Minister Uri Ariel.

Tekuma has been arguing that it's a question of values, reportedly complaining, "Bennett is afraid to discuss the character and values of the party," etc, alleging that, "he prefers to split the religious Zionist world and sell (out) its values and the settlers just to gather some more votes from Yesh Atid." And now there are those influential figures who are actually calling for a split, with the suggested option of postponing possible unity until after the elections. Speaking on Galei Yisrael, Rabbi Elyakim Levanon, Dean of the Elon Moreh Yeshiva, is promoting that very possibility, saying, "Unity does not mean confusion," and adding, "Unity of too many topics on one platform brings in the end chaos. When one wants to paint a picture he doesn't mix colors. Each color needs to have its own place."

In the old system of one mandate parties, that may have been true, but in the new system in which 3.25% of the vote is needed to even get into the Knesset, such an argument is near-sighted. The national religious world has seen many break-off parties, sometimes over small differences in political strategy and often over minor disagreements about issues. In every case of a split, the cause has been weakened and the national religious public ends up having to stop traffic on the highways and risking arrest through civil disobedience to have their voices heard.

We are standing at a crossroads at which we can go back to the those sad days of two or three small right-wing parties or perhaps worse, a situation in which one or more won't pass the Knesset threshold and tens of thousands of valuable votes or more will be wasted.

A large Bayit Yehudi, according to most polls, has the potential to be the second largest party, which would virtually assure a rightward shift in national priorities. If Tekuma really believes that its values and goals are appreciated by the national religious public, it should stop demanding guaranteed places on the candidates list and should run in the party primaries like everyone else. I have yet to hear a valid reason why Tekuma candidates shouldn't have to compete and non-Tekuma candidates should. The candidates should voice their positions on the issues and tell us about their qualifications to be effective Knesset members.

Trust the national religious and traditional public to decide in the primary who its candidates will be, and that, too, will bring the voters in the general election. The people want unity and peace in the Jewish Home, but they also want to choose their own leadership. Let the people choose.

Moshe Kahlon – The Next Yair Lapid?

"Popularity should be no scale for the election of politicians. If it would depend on popularity, Donald Duck and The Muppets would take seats in Senate."

(Orson Welles, American actor, director, writer, and producer)

In almost every Israeli election in recent years, there arises a new center party, anointed with supposedly unique, yet moderate qualities that the media praises as the rising political power to be reckoned with. Two years ago, it was the Yesh Atid party, established by one Yair Lapid, which took the political scene by storm, suddenly becoming the second largest party in Israel.

In this new election season, the latest superstar creating this year's new and improved centrist party is former Likud Minister of Communications Moshe Kahlon. Kahlon was a very popular Likudnik, at least until he temporarily left politics, apparently dissatisfied with Prime Minister Binyamin Netanyahu's failure to reward his popularity with an appropriate position of stature in the party.

Kahlon has claimed that he left the Likud because of the lack of sufficient emphasis on socioeconomic issues, which he considers to be his strong suit. As Communications Minister, he was responsible for successfully breaking up the monopoly in the cellular telephone industry, impressively using competition in the free market to lower prices for the consumer. Now in his position as leader of a new centrist party, Kahlon is promising to extend those reforms to banking and other industries in which monopolies still hold sway.

Breaking up monopolies should have been vintage Netanyahu, but the nation's leading politician, who happens to be a very knowledgeable MIT-trained economist, seemingly wasn't willing to take on the oligarchs at the ensconced banking, (regular) telephone, and electric industries, an admittedly awesome task that could create labor chaos and temporary or prolonged disruptions of service. That being the case, or at least the public perception, Netanyahu left open the playing field for a Moshe Kahlon to portray himself as the potential socioeconomic savior, having made his name by trumpeting the capitalist virtues of competition and the free market.

Unfortunately for Kahlon, man does not live on bread alone, and a national candidate must address controversial foreign policy issues. Now that he is a candidate and a centrist one at that, he wants to appeal to the Left as well as to the Right, and for that reason, he seems to be making an intentional shift from his former professed loyalty to the Land of Israel. Speaking in a Tel Aviv pub yesterday, Kahlon showed that he is perfectly willing to part with parts of the biblical heartland of Israel:

> "I am a former member of the Likud, a real Likud that knows how to achieve peace, that knows how to give up land," Kahlon proclaimed. "My friends and I will not miss a chance for peace. I believe we must act on that front."

Sounds a bit like his former boss in the Likud, or even further left. Ever wonder why Israel has such bad international public relations? A country that is so willing to surrender its most historical places for a promise of peace by those who are holding a gun to our heads cannot win the public relations battle. It's worthwhile to remember that the State of Israel was established in 1948, not for the purpose of peace, but for the purpose of reestablishing Jewish sovereignty in its ancient homeland. Someone should point that out to Kahlon, lest he continue to declare his lack of faithfulness to the Land of Israel in order to get votes from the left side of the political spectrum.

Economics and social mobility are important values, but the Land of Israel is eternal. The purpose of our return to the land in fulfillment of prophecy wasn't and isn't just to create a thriving economy. That may be a nice result of the return to the land and the consequent free expression of Jewish creativity and initiative, but economics alone is not the goal. Resettling, rebuilding, and spreading the light of Torah from the entire Land of Israel in fulfillment of prophecy is the goal. Hopefully, Kahlon will remember that on his next visit to the local bar.

Israel's Center-Left Bloc?

"The most dangerous of all falsehoods is a slightly distorted truth."

(Georg Christoph Lichtenberg, German scientist, philosopher, and satirist)

In every election year, we read in the news about the "Rightist Bloc" led by the Likud party and about the "Center-Left Bloc" led by the Labor party. All of the pre-election polls refer to these two voting blocs as fairly evenly divided. The usually unspoken-about problem is that those who are identified as "Center-Left" are really not centrist or moderate."

As Chairman of the Jordan Valley Regional Council David Elhayani recently told Arutz Sheva, "This is an election campaign in which we need to decide between left and right, and make no mistake; there is no center here, that's only a word of media advisers."

In other words, the mainstream media in Israel and elsewhere, which is mainly dominated by the Left, inaccurately calls the leftists "centrists" in order to help them get votes. Voters who aren't ideologically inclined will feel more comfortable voting for a centrist than a leftist or a rightist. That's why the Center-Right Bloc, led by the Likud, is never identified by the mainstream media as even leaning center, since that might attract voters.

Putting economic and religious issues to the side, what do the terms Right and Left actually mean in Israel? The Right should be accurately defined as at least resisting withdrawals from parts of the Land of Israel and opposing the creation of an Islamic terrorist state in Judea, Samaria, and eastern

Jerusalem (the biblical heartland of Israel). The Left should accurately be defined as advocating forced building freezes on Jews in Judea, Samaria, and eastern Jerusalem, as well as calling for the destruction of Jewish communities there and the establishment of a Hamas-Fatah (Palestinian Authority) independent state in their stead.

So what is the reality? Are the heads of the "Center-Left Bloc" really just centrists who in some cases lean left on socioeconomic issues? Let's check the positions of the leaders of the relevant political parties on the existential issue of land and peace:

- Yitzhak Herzog (Labor) – in favor of creating a Hamas-Fatah (Palestinian Authority) independent state in Judea and Samaria and eastern Jerusalem

- Yair Lapid (Yesh Atid) – withheld security funding for Jewish communities in Judea and Samaria, in favor of a building freeze in Judea and Samaria

- Tzipi Livni (HaTnuah) – in favor of creating a Hamas-Fatah (Palestinian Authority) independent state in Judea and Samaria and eastern Jerusalem

- Moshe Kahlon (Kulanu) – in favor of "giving up land" and presumably giving it to the Hamas-Fatah (Palestinian Authority) independent state in Judea and Samaria and eastern Jerusalem

- Avigdor Liberman (Yisrael Beytenu) – in favor of giving the Palestinian Authority significant sections of pre-1967 Israel – e.g. parts of the Negev and "the Triangle" (lower Galilee), "in exchange" for parts of Judea and Samaria.

What the politicians cited above are advocating are all left-wing positions, well in line with the failed "Land for Peace" formula. "Land for Peace" was designed to create two states, Israel and Palestine, that would live side-by-side in peace. Sadly, that violently burst bubble, an illusion created by the peace profiteers, has only brought death and destruction in its wake, turning thousands of Israelis into terror victims. Has Israel gone astray to such an extent that those who promote such national suicide are considered centrists?

Buji Herzog Wimps Out

"A lot of people are afraid to tell the truth, to say no. That's where toughness comes into play. Toughness is not being a bully. It's having backbone."

(Robert Kiyosaki, American author and businessman)

Yitzhak (Buji) Herzog comes from a distinguished family. His grandfather, of blessed memory, was Chief Rabbi Yitzhak Halevy Herzog. His father, MK and eventually President Chaim Herzog, was a respected man of integrity, but had moved away from his father's religiosity and worldview, aligning himself with the left-wing secular Labor party. His son, nicknamed Buji, has continued that new family tradition, becoming a Labor party MK and recently being anointed its leader, hence its candidate for Prime Minister.

The problem with Buji Herzog is that while he may be a nice guy, he has never been known for his toughness, and that deficiency has become quite evident in the pact that he just signed with former Justice Minister Tzipi Livni, thereby saving her sinking HaTnuah party ship from political extinction. By most accounts, poor Tzipi, the hapless lead negotiator in the failed peace process, who still refuses to admit her obsequious behavior running after Mahmoud Abbas and Saeb Erekat, was not going to get enough votes in the upcoming election to even make it back into the Knesset.

Livni had started conveniently shifting to the left of the political spectrum back in 2005, fleeing the Likud for a cushy position in Ariel Sharon's new left of center Kadima party, which he had established specifically to enable the mass expulsion of Jews from Gaza and northern Samaria, followed by the annihilation of those communities. After Kadima, with its strange assortment of opportunists and corrupt egos self-destructed, following its leader's indictment on suspicion of multiple crimes, Livni formed her own HaTnuah, another odd concoction of political refugees, with strong left-wing inclinations and six seats in the previous Knesset. She has now moved further leftward, rushing into Buji's arms, but it should come as no surprise. Tzipi Livni is no fool and her survival skills are much stronger than her political principles. Due to Buji's basic sense of kindness, which he no doubt inherited from his saintly grandfather, Tzipi has been rescued from having to spend the rest of her life as an ordinary citizen outside of the Knesset. But that's not all – now she becomes number two on the Labor party list of candidates and, if Labor somehow wins the election and forms the next coalition, she gets to become prime minister at midterm, in musical chairs rotation with the Labor party leader.

What is the significance of all this for the average voter? Firstly, the deal between Herzog and Livni reveals both an incredible lack of wise judgment, and especially, a lack of toughness on Herzog's part. According to most polls, Labor was predicted to get a relatively impressive 15-19 seats in the upcoming elections. The addition of Livni and the other leftist opportunists from HaTnuah may seem to add a few mandates at this early stage, but pre-election polls are very fickle, and the addition of a party of proven losers to the Labor list doesn't bode well for its success.

The real problem for Herzog's campaign is that if he is capable of negotiating such a bad deal with Tzipi Livni, what will he do opposite the Americans and the European Union? All the more so, when ceasefire pressures are applied at the end of the next war, how will he confront Fatah, Hamas, or any other shrewd Islamic terrorist organization? If he caves in so pathetically when negotiating opposite a sagging Tzipi Livni who was on her way to political oblivion, how will he protect Israel's interests when confronted by the likes of Barack Obama, Khaled Mashal, or Hassan Nasrallah?

Buji might be a nice guy, but can we really trust his weakness and naivety opposite the dangers of the world?

Responding To The PA –
Liberman's Plan Of Weakness

"Speak softly and carry a big stick."

(Theodore Roosevelt, American President)

W hen trying to be tough, is it sometimes better not to say anything?

Responding to the repeated Palestinian Authority (PA) "political attacks" on Israel, including attempts to obtain recognition of "Palestine" as an independent state in the UN Security Council and in other international forums, Foreign Minister Avigdor Liberman has once again announced that Israel shouldn't just sit and complain, but should be proactive. In doing so, he laid out parameters for what steps need to be taken by Israel to counter the hostile actions taken by the PA, which are in clear violation of the Oslo "Peace" Accords.

So what were the tough words that Liberman actually said? He began by stating the following:

> "The State of Israel will not agree to be dictated to by the Palestinians. Any attempt by the Palestinians, assisted by international bodies, to impose on us their desired solution, will only deteriorate the situation in the region even more and be liable to fail."

Given these strong statements by Mr. Liberman, one might have expected him to follow up with some similarly strong actions that will be taken by Israel, so as not to allow the aggressors to achieve, as he put it, "their desired solution". Perhaps calling for a government decision to declare the

Oslo Accords null and void? Perhaps adopting a Cabinet decision that Israel will no longer accept the validity of the Palestinian Authority? Perhaps at the very least, ending security cooperation?

The surprising answer? None of the above – Liberman called for the adoption of his peace proposal, according to which Israel would totally withdraw from the relatively large region in east-central Israel known as the Triangle, in which several hundred thousand Arab citizens of Israel live. In exchange, Israel would retain most of the Jewish populated communities in Judea and in Samaria, areas that are already in Israel's possession, but where Israeli sovereignty has not yet been declared.

In short, the Liberman plan gives the Arabs sovereignty in a central part of Israel that is not in their possession and that is legally under Israel's sovereignty, "in exchange" for central parts of Israel that already are in our possession, and in which we can declare sovereignty tomorrow without striking any deal with the Hamas-Fatah PA. Does Liberman's plan sound like a fair deal? Is that really the tough action that he seemed to call for in response to the PA's political attacks on Israel?

The Liberman plan gives them exactly what they want – continued Israeli withdrawal from the Land of Israel. Liberman does justify his plan by pointing to the demographic threat from the Arabs, but in our present reality of a rising Jewish birthrate and a shrinking Arab one, claims of an existential demographic threat to Israel's existence are no longer, if they ever were, a convincing reason to surrender land to our enemies.

As if to convince us that his plan has merit, Liberman goes on to explain that world leaders (who, by the way, are always pressuring Israel to hand over land for the promise of peace) don't even object to his plan:

"I have never heard a rejection of this idea when I put it in front of world leaders."

Yes, the "land for peace" cheerleaders around the world actually seem to like this plan. Is that Liberman's rationale for withdrawal from the center of Israel? Let's not be fooled again – the Liberman plan is a pathetic diplomatic surrender that will be interpreted as weakness in the Arab countries and in the broader Islamic world. It will also legitimize the Arab demands for sovereignty in the adjacent Galilee region. In the upcoming elections, it may bring Liberman a few votes from the Left or even a few more votes from Arabs, but it's no less dangerous than the Oslo Accords, and maybe even more so. Hopefully, the voters will recognize that.

The Tomb Of Samuel –
Who Is Sovereign?

*"There are natural and imprescriptible rights which
an entire nation has no right to violate."*

(Marquis de Lafayette,
French aristocrat and military officer, who played
a pivotal role in both the American and French Revolutions)

Israel is being verbally blasted by leading Islamic religious figures after the Civil Administration in Judea and Samaria announced its intention to renovate the Tomb of Samuel, the burial site of the great judge and leader of ancient Israel, Samuel the Prophet. The site is located just north of Jerusalem, even though Samuel grew up in Shiloh in the heart of Samaria (in the so-called West Bank).

Senior Muslim cleric Sheikh Yusuf Adeis has referred to the planned renovation as "religious persecution being carried out by the Israeli government on Islamic and Christian holy sites in Palestine."

Lest anyone think that this proposed renovation might actually be a case of religious persecution, the question must be asked: What is really bugging these Muslims?

To understand the answer, it's worthwhile to pay some attention to the building of other Islamic "places of worship", especially in the Land of Israel, but it would be instructive to start with one such site in New York City. Many Americans were shocked a few years ago by the announcement of "The Cordoba Initiative", a worldwide Islamic effort to raise funds for the construction of a fifteen story mosque and Islamic cultural center next to Ground Zero in Manhattan, the site of one of the worst Islamic terrorist attacks in history.

The name of the project was not without significance. Cordoba was the city in southern Spain where the first great mosque in Spain was built at the onset of the Islamic conquest in the eighth century. It also served as a symbol of this conquest, as the great mosque in Cordoba had been symbolically built on the foundations of a large Christian Cathedral that the Muslims had destroyed.

One historical fact that many folks in the West are unaware of is that Muslims have always built their mosques on the ruins of historically significant sites of other religions. This is to show their sovereignty and the triumph of Islam over all of the people who they refer to in the Koran as "the unbelievers."

Several poignant examples:

- The Temple Mount – The massive Islamic Dome of the Rock structure was built on top of the ruins of the Holy Temple of Israel in Jerusalem.

- The Cave of the Patriarchs – The large prayer area in Hebron that the Muslims call the Ibrahimi Mosque, today dominates the site that the biblical father of Israel, Abraham, bought to bury his wife Sarah, and where the Patriarchs of Israel and most of the Matriarchs of Israel are buried.

- Samuel's Tomb – A large mosque complex was built above and around the tiny room that houses the tomb of Samuel the Prophet.

If Israel was to destroy any of the above "Islamic" sites, which were all built illegally as an invasion of Jewish holy sites, it would be standing on firm moral ground. Obviously, this won't be done in the near future due to the international political ramifications, as perceived by Israel's current political leadership, but it would certainly be an historical correction of a severe injustice perpetrated by Islam.

However, that's not what we're talking about here. Simply renovating Samuel's Tomb is an absolutely minimal exercise of Israel taking responsibility as the sovereign authority for a religious, historical site that needs renovation. The Islamic savages may scream and yell and complain about persecution, but if their ruckus turns into riots or attempts at terrorism, they should be crushed with no hesitation. There is only one legitimate sovereign authority in the Land of Israel and it is indeed an act of folly to be merciful towards those who are making religious war against us on every level.

It would be wise to remember that Samuel the Prophet made the ultimate statement about asserting Israeli sovereignty, by appointing the first two kings of Israel – Saul and then David, who united the Land of Israel under Israel's sovereignty, some 1,500 years before Islam was invented. That lesson about asserting sovereignty should be heeded today, as well.

The Next Netanyahu Coalition: Waiting for Answers

"We all wear masks and the time comes when we cannot remove them without removing some of our own skin."

(Andre Berthiaume, French author)

Deputy Environmental Protection Minister Ofir Akunis (Likud) has a lot to say about what Israel's response should be to the Palestinian Authority's hostile diplomatic moves at the United Nations (UN) and at the International Criminal Court (ICC). Akunis, a close ally of Prime Minister Binyamin Netanyahu in the Likud, recently remarked that "we have to take off the kid gloves." The response to the moves, according to Akunis, is that "we need to apply sovereignty on Judea and Samaria. Their unilateral move needs to be hit by a clear response – applying sovereignty and pushing settlement."

Furthermore, Akunis sharply criticized Tzipi Livni, co-leader of the leftist Labor-HaTnuah party, claiming that she is still obsessed by the illusion of a peace partner on the so-called Palestinian side:

> "I don't trust her. She will never admit to her failure (as peace negotiator). She said that we need to sit in a room and talk even when she knew that it was impossible. There's no peace partner on the other side," said the deputy minister.

While it's hard to disagree with his criticism of Livni and while his proposed response to the PA's moves at the UN and the ICC is certainly reasonable, one has to wonder if he has consulted his boss in the Likud, who is disturbingly silent about his own lack of a response to the PA's diplomatic aggression. Especially now, during an election campaign, the public deserves to know which Bibi Netanyahu it will be getting – the one who has warned many times that PA diplomatic aggression towards Israel in international bodies will be met with a strong Israeli response – or the one that has called for the two-state solution, otherwise known as "land for peace".

The sad fact is that since his first term as PM, Netanyahu's Zionist actions have never lived up to his Zionist words, not in the realm of settlement, not in his indecisive role as commander-in-chief of the military, nor in his lack of resolve in rejecting diplomatic hostility with more than words.

Obviously, the Tzipi Livni-Yitzhak Herzog team on the Left is far worse, as is Yair Lapid, but if Likud wins and Netanyahu succeeds in forming the next coalition, we the voters need to know the answers to these three questions:

1.   Would the next Netanyahu-led coalition be urged by its leader to adopt the Levy Report, which affirmed the historic legality of Jewish settlement in Judea and Samaria?

2.   Would the next Netanyahu-led coalition consider dissolving the PA as a sensible response to PA sponsored terrorism and diplomatic aggression against Israel?

3.   Would the next Netanyahu-led coalition end the unannounced freeze on the granting of housing permits for Jews in Jerusalem, Judea, and Samaria?

The election is on March 17. Waiting for answers…

Supply & Demand, Not Cheap Politics

"In politics, stupidity is not a handicap."

(Napoleon Bonaparte,
French military and political leader)

In most election seasons, the "lame-duck" administration doesn't make many important decisions, unless there is a foreign policy crisis. Today was an exception.

In a wise common sense decision, the Israeli Cabinet approved a plan to move several IDF bases to free up large swathes of valuable real estate, for the purpose of enabling large-scale building of housing in the center of the country. This bold move, in which the bases will be relocated to the Negev desert, will be a boon to the economy in the southern regions, as well, as thousands of soldiers will bring new economic life to some of the neglected towns in the periphery.

For many months, former Finance Minister Yair Lapid (Yesh Atid) has been hurling mud at Prime Minister Binyamin Netanyahu (Likud) and at everyone else who has dared to criticize his 0% VAT plan that would give a large tax-reduction to first-time home-buyers. While targeted tax reduction has its uses in the right circumstances, the Lapid plan was a populist bluff from the get-go. The Cabinet decision puts the real issue on the table for all to see in action. The real issue, which Lapid should have learned in Economy 101, if he ever took such a basic course, is called "supply and demand".

The basic concept is that housing prices rise when the demand for homes outstrips the supply of available housing. On the other hand, when the supply is increased by significantly enabling the building of new housing, the demand for such housing is reduced, and prices naturally fall.

Netanyahu, as a knowledgeable economist, has known this for years, but has often allowed his political calculations to get in the way of what needs to be done to create real competition and economic activity in the marketplace. Inappropriate politically-based decisions have lead to the anti-growth building freeze in Judea, in Samaria, and in Jerusalem, as well as the failure to confront monopolies, among other economic blunders. Finance Minister Lapid, who carried a lot of weight in the previous administration, clearly played a role in some of these bad decisions and to this very day, he flaunts his ignorance, insisting that 0% VAT is a way of lowering housing prices. Prime Minister Netanyahu is to be commended for apparently changing the direction.

Hopefully, the latest Cabinet decision will be a harbinger of sensible change that will open up the housing market, spurring renewed economic growth throughout the country, including the vast underdeveloped areas of the Negev, the Galilee, the Golan Heights, Samaria, and Judea, as well as encouraging a building boom in Israel's capital, Jerusalem.

Feiglin's Delusions of Grandeur: Past and Future

"The belief that one's own view of reality is the only reality is the most dangerous of all delusions."

(Paul Watzlawick, Austrian psychologist)

After several failed campaigns for the leadership of the Likud, followed by his latest failure to even win election to the Likud's slate of candidates for the upcoming elections, MK Moshe Feiglin has officially resigned from the Likud. As a response to this rejection, such a move could be expected, but in an ironic twist of direction, Feiglin is now promising "to continue the path of real Jewish leadership" by establishing a new political party.

Interviewed today on the "Galei Yisrael" radio station, Feiglin was asked if he might be interested in running as a candidate in one of the existing faith-based parties that are loyal to the land and heritage of Israel. He replied that he wasn't interested, that what is important is not the party, rather its vision, and therefore he plans to form his own party.

One has to wonder what he is talking about and why. For nearly twenty years, Feiglin has been endlessly promoting the concept of influencing the political process from within the ruling party, the Likud. Often denouncing the smaller sectarian/nationalistic parties, he boldly proclaimed that he would achieve his national-religious objectives and achieve leadership within the Likud. Not satisfied with simply becoming a member of Knesset and increasing the national-religious membership in a party that was not religious at its ideological core, Feiglin inexplicably declared that he would eventually become the leader of the Likud, and he ran several expensive, but failed campaigns to achieve that objective.

To now establish a new political party and to say that "this is a continuation of the mission" sounds disingenuous and even hypocritical. In the above interview, Feiglin even disparaged those who told him that starting a new political party would split the national-religious vote, even though this is in fact what it would do.

The tragic irony is that the great champion of the "big party system" has taken a 180-degree turn, as a result of his personal failure to get reelected. To his credit, Feiglin's policy goals have always been serious and consistent, and he has proven himself effective at explaining and getting publicity for those views, but his grand political strategy to change and take over the Likud from within has been a disaster. Despite a slight rightward shift in the composition of the party over the past few years, the Likud has remained basically the same Likud that talks about the land of Israel, yet freezes Jewish building in Judea, Samaria, and Jerusalem; that threatens the Palestinian Authority, yet doesn't follow through on those threats; that starts wars, but doesn't follow through or allow the IDF to win decisive victories.

Feiglin's personal and political disappointment is certainly understandable. However, his sudden strategic shift, which seems to be based on a politician's personal interest more than anything else, is irresponsible, and it is that which he should reconsider if he truly is looking to actualize "the vision."

The Islamic Tsunami Strikes Again

"It's one thing to say, 'I don't like what you said to me and I find it rude and offensive,' but the moment you threaten violence in return, you've taken it to another level, where you lose whatever credibility you had."

(Salman Rushdie, British Indian novelist)

Twelve people have been murdered in Paris in a vicious terrorist attack in the offices of a newspaper. What was their crime? They dared to publish satirical cartoons about Islam.

Obviously, the rapidly increasing Muslim population in France is feeding the voracious Islamic appetite to gradually conquer Europe through terrorist intimidation, to be followed by demographic dominance. In my book, "The Islamic Tsunami", I speak of two Islamic tsunamis. The first is the tsunami of terrorism, which is designed to frighten people into submission (which is the literal meaning of the word Islam), so that they will be afraid to speak out about the second tsunami, quieter but more ominous – the plan that is being gradually implemented, to change Western civilization into an Islamic caliphate.

The terrorist attack in Paris is a clear example of this strategy, which is shared by all of the Islamic fundamentalist ideologues of all shades and hues. These ideologues are represented by and/or work in coordination with the multiple Islamic terrorist organizations, such as Islamic Jihad, Hamas (in partnership with Fatah), ISIS, Boko Haram, Al Qaeda, Muslim Brotherhood, Hezbollah, Taliban, and all the others.

Furthermore, France and the EU need to understand that the Islamic world perceives political pandering to their demands as weakness, and pounces on it with a vengeance.

Case in point, this sequence of recent events:

- December 2014 – France's lower house of parliament votes 339 to 151 to recognize "State of Palestine".
- December 2014 – The European Union Court removes Hamas from its terrorist list.
- December 2014 – The European Parliament adopts a resolution recognizing Palestinian statehood in principle.
- December 2014 – France Votes for Palestine sovereignty deadline resolution in the UN Security Council.

Warning: These repeated acts of appeasement will encourage and embolden the enemies of freedom and the friends of Jihad. The terror threat will increase proportionately with each act of Western weakness and the pathetic pandering to Islamic demands.

In France And Elsewhere: Terrorism Is Not An Enemy

"What really alarms me about President Bush's 'War on Terrorism' is the grammar. How do you wage war on an abstract noun? How is 'Terrorism' going to surrender? It's well known, in philological circles, that it's very hard for abstract nouns to surrender."

(Terry Jones, Welsh comedian, screenwriter and actor)

Like so many others, the European Jewish Congress, which is the official representative body for Jewish communities in Europe, is seriously off target in its calls to battle "Terrorism."

"Europe is at war with an ideology that seeks mass bloodshed and murder," said the organization's president, Dr. Moshe Kantor.

And what is that ideology called?

The answer: "Terrorism."

He goes on to explain that we are not in "a war against Muslims or Islam, but against a radical interpretation which targets for death anyone that they decide is the enemy, including journalists and Jews, but all are potential targets." Not missing a beat, French President Francois Hollande referred to "fanatics who have nothing to do with the Muslim religion."

Apparently, at least according to these European leaders, the way to combat the ongoing scourge of attacks in France, is not by fighting against the religion which has as its core belief the obligation of "Jihad", or holy war against non-Muslims. Presumably the battle will be waged against "Terrorism."

However, terrorism is not an enemy. It is a strategy that

is openly justified by Jihad, the core ideology of Islam.

If France and the rest of Europe are to have any realistic hope of saving themselves from the Islamic tsunami that threatens to soon engulf them, they need to be clear in their identification of the challenge:

The followers of the ideology of Jihad, which lies at the core of Islam, are using terrorism as a strategy to achieve their goal of world domination. Both the strategy and its underlying ideology need to be defeated. In order to succeed, this struggle will have to be fought on many levels – militarily, educationally, and politically – ruthlessly hunting down terrorists and their leadership, taking critical legal steps to prevent the spread of Islamic ideology, and hermetically sealing borders, except for those Muslims who want to leave.

There are many other steps needed, but that is beyond the scope of this specific article.

And to the Jews of France: Your situation is far more precarious at the moment than the rest of your imperiled countrymen. The ground in France is burning under your feet, but you do have where to go. It's time to finally come to your real home and you will be welcomed as family here in Israel!

Mahmoud Abbas to the World: Je Suis Terroriste!

"Well, first he's in the background, and then he's in the front ... Both eyes are looking like they're on a rabbit hunt ... Nobody can see through him ... No, not even the Chief of Police ... You know that sometimes Satan comes as a man of peace."

(Bob Dylan, musician, songwriter)

Palestinian Authority President Mahmoud Abbas is going to the Je Suis Charlie rally in Paris, joining other world leaders protesting the recent terror attacks in France. His appearance is at the invitation of the French government, which doesn't seem to have learned anything.

It's certainly comforting to know that Abbas feels the pain of the French people. Maybe he will also start to feel the pain of the Holocaust survivors who know about his Nazi-excusing doctoral dissertation, or maybe he will suddenly and inexplicably stop naming streets and public squares after "Palestinian" Muslims who have killed thousands of Jewish civilians?

I guess that many of us Israelis are too cynical for our own good. At least that's what bleeding heart leftists like Tzipi Livni or Buji Herzog would tell us. Believe it or not, that's what often happens when you and your family members and countless friends, neighbors, and teachers are killed or wounded by Abbas's foot soldiers.

Okay, okay, let's give him the benefit of the doubt and we will assume that Abbas (who we can affectionately call "Abu Mazen" to show that he really is a regular guy), will be coming to Paris with tried and true, constructive ideas for the peace process. Perhaps he will suggest that France start bankrolling the terrorists as he has been doing for years, giving millions of dollars every year to Islamic terrorists and their families for terrorist attacks committed against Israelis. Let us point out, for all of you "liberals" out there, that Abbas happens to be an equal opportunity employer – He supports not only his own Fatah terrorists, but also Hamas, Islamic Jihad, ISIS, Al Qaeda, and any other human-rights loving Jihadist terrorists.

Could it be that Abbas will bring with him to Paris some of his peace-loving world leader friends from the UN Human Rights Council – perhaps from "progressive" countries like Saudi Arabia, Cuba, or Venezuela?

Netanyahu in Paris: Representing Israel with Honor

"The task of leadership is not to put greatness into humanity, but to elicit it, for the greatness is already there."

(John Buchan, Scottish politician)

Anyone who reads this blog with any regularity is well aware that Prime Minister Binyamin (Bibi) Netanyahu has very often received sharp criticism in these pages on a variety of issues. These have ranged from his unfortunate penchant for making empty threats, to his reluctance to go forward with the necessary rebuilding of the biblical heartland of Israel.

That being said, when the political leader of Israel went to Paris as Israel's chief representative after the horrific terror attacks in recent days, he deserved the unified support of his people, and therefore, the harsh criticism leveled towards Netanyahu from his political foes, including former Finance Minister Yair Lapid (Yesh Atid) and Tzipi Livni (Zionist Union), was especially bizarre and unfair, even if it is election season. This wasn't a question of disagreements about policy issues, which are certainly fair game, but it wasn't Netanyahu's policies that were being debated by his critics. It was simply cheap political sniping.

Netanyahu was traveling not just as the political leader of the State of Israel, but also of the Zionist movement and the Jewish People. Furthermore, Israel is the unofficial leader of the free world in the war on Islamic terrorism and so our Prime Minister's presence on the front lines of the march of millions in Paris was very appropriate. We can disagree on any myriad of issues, but Bibi was cheered in the Grand Synagogue in Paris, because, as the symbol of Israel that he is, he was there to stand with the suffering Jews of France in their hour of pain. He admirably and sensitively walked the fine line between showing sympathy, understanding, and support, while simultaneously urging them to make Aliyah to Israel.

By going to Paris and in the dignified manner in which he did, Netanyahu showed that he understands the international importance of his role as Prime Minister of the Jewish State. For that he should be receiving compliments, not embarrassing personal attacks from Israel's pathetic coterie of whining leftists.

Shas's Enabler of Oslo:
Aryeh Deri Returns

"They judged him in court. Why take someone who is a thief? Why would you take someone who accepts bribes?"

(Rabbi Ovadia Yosef, leading Torah sage, expressing his opposition to restoring Aryeh Deri as leader of the Shas)

The great enabler of the Oslo Peace Accords, which should more accurately be called the Oslo Terror Accords, has officially returned as the head of the Shas party. Aryeh Deri, who tricked Shas spiritual leader Rabbi Ovadia Yosef (according to the rabbi himself) into letting Shas support the suicidal Oslo "peace" process in past governing coalitions, has now returned with the same arrogance that he had when he headed the formerly powerful Sephardic Haredi (ultra-Orthodox) party, typically justifying his past sins by accusing others:

"Today, there is no partner for peace. Up to now, those who gave back communities and parts of the land of Israel were mostly right-wing governments, so please do not preach morality to us."

Today there is no partner for peace? Who was the partner back then, when Deri supported the corrupt "peace" process that left thousands of maimed Jewish bodies and pools of blood in the streets of Jerusalem and throughout the Land of Israel?

While it's apparently true that Prime Minister Binyamin Netanyahu carried out withdrawals because his hands were bound by signed agreements that he had inherited ... and while it is apparently true that Prime Minister Ariel Sharon carried out withdrawals in order to appease the left-wing establishment and avoid prosecution for his and his sons' personal corruption ... what is *absolutely true* is that, as a partner in successive governments, both right-wing and left-wing, Shas did not oppose successive withdrawals and expulsions of Jews from parts of the Land of Israel ... thereby enabling the terrible waves of terrorism that left thousands of Israelis killed or wounded.

Aryeh Deri's hands are still drenched with that blood. According to the late spiritual leader of Shas, Rabbi Ovadia Yosef, Deri deceived him, coercing him into not opposing the Oslo Accords in the governing coalition, thereby enabling its passage, then supported the subsequent withdrawals, which further unleashed the vicious waves of terrorism on the average Israeli that Deri now claims to care for.

Don't be fooled by his black hat, ostensibly symbolizing religious piety. The mask of the leftist wheeler-dealer Aryeh Deri has been removed by the recently-exposed video interview with Rabbi Yosef. In that video, the revered Torah scholar blasted the convicted Deri for his political corruption, his leftist views, and his deception.

After the unrepentant Deri was let out of jail, Rabbi Yosef went against his better judgment by keeping his previously-made promise allowing Deri to return as the head of Shas, thereby betraying the quietly loyal Eli Yishai, who had led Shas with a steady hand in Deri's absence. It's no wonder that Yishai, along with many of his supporters, has recently left Shas to form his own party, Ha'Am Itanu, leaving Deri's deception and left-leaning party behind him.

Given all of the above, it should be clear that anyone who votes for Aryeh Deri's Shas in the upcoming elections is supporting a continuation of his horrible legacy – of corruption, of suicidal peace plans, and of the resulting terrorism and loss of lives.

Is Netanyahu Damaging United States-Israel Relations?

"Moses said to the people, 'Do not fear! Stand firm and see the salvation of the Lord that He will provide for you today.' "

(Exodus 14:13-14)

It seems almost like a recurring mantra. Once again, in this latest election campaign, Prime Minister Binyamin Netanyahu of the Likud party is being lambasted by his leftist political opponents. This time the political fireballs are being hurled by the inaccurately-named Zionist Camp party of Yitzhak (Buji) Herzog and Tzipi Livni. The Buji-Tzipi team is blaming Netanyahu for "ruining Israel's relationship with its best ally, the United States." More specifically, the post-Zionist couple and their allies in the left-wing media have been shedding crocodile tears about the tension between Netanyahu and Obama, Netanyahu and Kerry, Netanyahu and Biden, and previously, Netanyahu and Hillary Clinton.

As annoying as the Buji-Tzipi carping may be, it would be foolish to whitewash the tensions as if they don't exist, or as if they don't matter. After all, we are talking about the elected government of the United States of America, which is the most important elected government that we have to deal with. Wouldn't it be far better if all were blissful and harmonious between our two countries?

However, while the tensions, and more importantly, the policy differences, are very real, it's critical that we take note of the fact that those tensions have been most evident with the Obama administration and with particularly hostile elements within the US State Department that are under President Obama's command. No doubt it is those same elements that have been responsible for the recent unfriendly statements expressed by the White House and State Department spokesmen, as well as the hostile actions recently carried out against Jewish communities in Samaria by American consulate officials based in Israel.

As distressing as those tensions may be, the United States does not consist of a monolithic populace that automatically kowtows to the whims and the foreign policy positions of its political leadership. It should be understood that despite the unpleasant stench emanating from the White House, there is tremendous support for Israel all across the great American heartland and along the coasts, and it even includes more than a few of Obama's Democrats, many of whom have sadly been intimidated by their executive leader from openly expressing their basic pro-Israel instincts.

Perhaps it was prompted by the chilling threat from ISIS or perhaps by the recent Islamic attacks in France, but the suppression of Congress by Obama's thought police is about to be rejected in the court of public opinion, as Prime Minister Netanyahu has just been invited as an honored guest to address a joint session of the two houses of Congress next month.

The White House reaction to the announced visit has been tepid at best, partially because the invitation came from House Speaker John Boehner, the Republican leader, whose party has been at odds with Obama. Furthermore, the GOP has been much more supportive of Israel in Congress than the Democrats have been, and certainly way more supportive than Obama and his friends in the State Department.

That being said, it's worth noting that President Obama's distress actually stems from more substantive policy issues. Obama has been consistently at loggerheads with Netanyahu over the American nuclear negotiations with the Islamic Republic of Iran, which has been toying with the Western powers in order to further its not-so-friendly nuclear aspirations. There have also been sharp disagreements on the Hamas-Fatah Palestinian issue and on Obama's obsessive refusal to identify Islamic terrorism as Islamic, thereby tying the hands of the Western powers. As any skilled hunter will tell you, if you can't correctly identify the beast, you can't defeat it.

The opportunity for Netanyahu to speak to Congress and to receive multiple standing ovations, even including many Democrats, will buttress Netanyahu's positions in his disagreements with the president. Furthermore, it will make the GOP look good and the Dems look bad, unless they join the Republican applause, and therefore, we should expect to see massive applause from both sides of the aisle.

Those are the main reasons why the Obama administration is so concerned about Netanyahu coming to Washington, but Bibi must go forward, and must do so unapologetically. A strong speech to Congress and, by extension, to the American people and the world, will strengthen Israel's crucial leadership role in the war on Islamic terrorism and will further improve an already solid relationship with the American people, the leader of the free world.

Will Obama be happy about this? Certainly not, but he will do his utmost not to reveal his displeasure, not publicly at least. Will the Israeli Left be happy? Also not, and they will seek to attack Netanyahu for political grandstanding. In any event, expect Obama's political henchmen to subsequently do his bidding, doing everything within their not-so-ethical power to interfere in the March 17 Israeli elections. As is known to all, this will be on behalf of the Buji-Tzipi post-Zionist cabal, which no doubt has already contacted the White House to request their assistance.

The "Zionist Camp" Misnomer

"Abuse of words has been the great instrument of sophistry and chicanery, of party, faction, and division of society."

(John Adams, American President)

When is a Zionist not a Zionist? The official name of the union of Yitzhak (Buji) Herzog and Tzipi Livni, combining their Labor and HaTnuah parties for the March 17 elections, has been interestingly announced as "The Zionist Camp". While there is no doubt that it sounds like a perfectly patriotic name worthy of praise, the question must be asked:

Is this false advertising?

After all, the Labor party of today is not the Labor party of David Ben-Gurion, who boldly declared, "What matters is not what the Goyim (Gentiles) say, but rather what the Jews do", or Golda Meir, who unapologetically remarked, "There is no Palestinian people".

Yes, those were the days, my friends, but Labor-HaTnuah is not made of the same ilk as the Labor Zionists of yesteryear. Let's read what some of the heavy hitters on the 2015 candidates list for Labor-HaTnuah say about Zionism:

Yitzhak (Buji) Herzog –

"The Jewish state expression is entirely mistaken, because it creates the impression of a nationality that enjoys excessive privileges."

Stav Shaffir –

"Hatikva is a racist national anthem."

Merav Michaeli –

"Women should not at all send their kids to the army when there is a continuous occupation for over 40 years."

Yossi Yonah –

"I don't connect to this word, Zionism. It doesn't express who I am."

Zuheir Bahloul –

"Our Palestinian identity is stronger than the Israeli one."

Need I say more? The so-called Zionist Camp of Labor-HaTnuah far better represents the philosophy of "Post-Zionism", which claims that by creating the State of Israel in 1948, Zionism had already accomplished its mission, and that there is no further need for the national anthem or the flag, nor is there a need for the law of return, or the imperative to resettle the historical Land of Israel.

While the misnomer, Zionist Camp, evokes proud images of blue and white, it doesn't reflect the disturbing views of its leadership, as stated in the representative samples above. Will the voters be fooled?

Winning Israel's Wars of Diplomacy

"In a time of universal deceit – telling the truth is a revolutionary act."

(George Orwell, British author)

For many years, it has been an open secret that Israel is losing the public relations war. This has been the case with Labor, Kadima, and yes, even Likud governments. Ever wonder why?

Israel's Ambassador to Switzerland, Yigal Caspi, as well as two other officials at Israeli embassies in India and France, recently expressed their public disapproval of Prime Minister Netanyahu's policies on Twitter. The appointed officials sharply criticized the leader of the government that they represent, for accepting an invitation to address Congress on the dangers of Iran's nuclear bomb program, as well as the subsequent tensions with the White House.

Several other very public messages from Israeli diplomats criticized Foreign Minister Avigdor Liberman for firing members of his Yisrael Beytenu party recently, as well as Economy Minister Naftali Bennett, calling him "messianic, violent, homophobic and anti-social."

As bizarre as it may be for Israeli diplomats to be publicly vilifying their own government's actions, even to the extent of vicious name-calling, the core of the problem actually lies much deeper. Consecutive Israeli governments, including those led by the Likud, have appointed as diplomats individuals who don't believe in Zionism as the national movement of the Jewish people, who see us as usurpers of "Palestinian land", who are anti-religious haters of Israel's biblical heritage, and whose connection to Israel is based solely on their birth in Israel, their army service, and/or their knowledge of the Hebrew language.

In that context, we can understand the ideological origins of such critical statements, coming as they do from individuals whose certificates and degrees in diplomacy, in addition to personal connections in the diplomatic ranks belie their often vacuous Jewish backgrounds. As unethical as it may be for a diplomat to rather undiplomatically criticize his or her own government, we need to remember where it's coming from.

Ultimately, the Likud-led government of Prime Minister Netanyahu has to take responsibility for this sorry state of affairs. When the government needs qualified people for various public jobs, it knows well how to broaden the market and encourage a wider range of individuals to apply for those positions. There are many other Israelis with a firm knowledge of Hebrew, English, and other languages, many of whom had made Aliyah from their native countries, but all of whom have impeccable Zionist credentials, including a love of the Land of Israel and a belief in the justice of our cause. Many of these individuals would no doubt welcome the opportunity to serve their country in public diplomacy.

Sadly, Foreign Minister Liberman, and his boss Mr. Netanyahu as well, have so far failed to bring enough new blood into Israel's diplomatic staff, and therefore, we will continue to lose the wars of diplomacy. Hopefully, the next government will act swiftly to rectify this problem.

Obama, Islam, and the Crusades

"Obama gets his identity and his ideology from his father."

(Dinesh D'Souza,
Indian-American political commentator, author)

US President Barack Obama has finally spoken out against the forces of religious extremism that are threatening all of Western civilization. In a speech to the National Prayer Breakfast, Obama, who up to this point has stubbornly refused to use the words "Islamic" and "terrorism" in the same breath, is finally criticizing an entire terrorist movement for its religious extremism.

Which one, you ask? ISIS perhaps?

Well, not exactly. While the leader of the free world could have aimed his arrows at a long list of Islamic terrorist organizations that compete fiercely in their barbarism – Hamas, Hezbollah, Al Qaeda, Boko Haram, and Islamic Jihad, to name but a few – he instead decided to identify what he considers to be the most shocking current manifestation of religious extremism, namely, the Christian Crusaders!

As an Israeli Jew with an acute sensitivity to what was done to my people throughout the ages, I am certainly aware of the extreme acts that were committed in the name of Christianity by the Crusaders. Yes, the Crusades were launched as a response to the brutal Muslim conquests, but many Jews were slaughtered as well. Furthermore, the Crusades led to centuries of religiously-justified persecution of the Jews all across Europe, including the Inquisition, when Jews suffered from mass expulsions, forced conversions, and far worse, and all in the name of Christianity.

However, the Crusades ended some 800 years ago.

Furthermore, it must be said that unlike Jihadist Muslims who are emulating the ways of Muhammad, such Christians weren't emulating Jesus, who wasn't known for beheadings or violent rampages.

Jumping back to the present, we see that the free world is being confronted with a variety of violent Islamic movements that have in common a strict adherence to the Islamic doctrine of Jihad, or holy war against non-Muslims (the unbelievers), which is arguably the highest precept in Islam, with abuse of women and children coming in a close second and third place. While many Christians in our times still believe that proselytizing is important, very few, if any, would call for the violent conversion of those who disagree with them, and certainly no Jews believe in such an intolerant, violent doctrine.

Barack Obama appears to have been so scarred from the unfortunate loss of his Muslim father at a young age that he can't recognize, nor admit, the real and present danger of the intolerant, violent Jihadist ideology and its deep roots in the core of Islam. It seems to be almost an infantile mantra: Islam not bad ... Islam not bad ... Islam not bad!

The problem is that as the leader of the free world, President Obama needs to be leading the fight against Islamic terrorism from ISIS to Iran. However, not only is he not doing it adequately, but he also gets in the way of those who are willing to lead. Rather than face the painful demons in his past, it's perhaps easier for him to point to the Crusaders of 800 years ago or to reference violent incidents in the Book of Deuteronomy (which he has done) to prove his specious point that Islam is no more dangerous than all the other religions. To face the "in your face" challenges of ISIS, Al Qaeda, Iran, Hamas, Taliban, Islamic Jihad, Fatah, Boko Haram, Hezbollah, and all the others, is much more difficult, and perhaps for Barack Hussein Obama, emotionally unbearable.

The Dems' Pro-Israel Litmus Test

"Iran is going to receive a sure path to nuclear weapons. Many of the restrictions that were supposed to prevent it from getting there will be lifted."

(Benjamin Netanyahu, Israeli Prime Minister)

Israeli Prime Minister Benjamin Netanyahu's upcoming speech to the joint houses of Congress has stirred up an unprecedented political storm in both Washington and Jerusalem, but there are several positive developments that are being overlooked by the media.

I have always emphasized that in the muddy world of politics, in which evasion and/or zig-zagging often seem to be the norm, the occasional emergence of clarification is a ray of light for the voting public.

Such a situation enabling clarification has developed as a result of the controversy over Netanyahu's expected March 3rd speech to Congress. While the Israeli Left has been mercilessly attacking Netanyahu for ignoring the wishes of the White House and for his insistence on going forward with the speech so close to the March 17 elections, their Democratic counterparts in Washington have been scrambling to decide what to do on the day of the speech.

The fact is that the Dems have a serious dilemma. Everyone knows that the controversy isn't really about the date of the Israeli elections, nor is it about the supposed lack of proper protocol in House Speaker John Boehner's invitation. The real issue is that there have been consistent reports in recent weeks, confirming that Iran and the Western powers are very close to signing an agreement. It has been reported that the proposed deal would enable the Islamic state to continue its drive to achieve full nuclear weapons capability. Netanyahu's speech to Congress couldn't be timelier in light of this existential threat to Israel's survival.

Most Democrats in Congress have long stressed their pro-Israel credentials, but they now need to decide whether to attend the speech, thereby literally standing firmly with Israel against Iran and the forces of Islamic extremism, or to be conveniently absent on that day, a prospect that House Minority Leader Nancy Pelosi has not so subtly hinted at. Such a conspicuous act by Democrats would be a demonstrative show of support for the Obama administration's policy of negotiating, or in the words of Iran's leadership, "begging" the mullahs in Teheran to sign an agreement.

Vice-President Joe Biden has already made it known that he is planning to be absent on the day of the speech, thereby supporting Obama's policy of weakness, and many of his congressional colleagues are now trying to decide what to do.

A word of warning to the Democrats: It's not enough to declare before every American election that you are pro-Israel, while spitting in its face in its time of need. The Democrats may not be happy about it, but their attendance at the Netanyahu speech will indeed be seen as a litmus test that pro-Israel American voters should take note of. The real question is: Are you for us or are you against us?

We will find out on March 3rd.

Bibi Comes Back to Samaria: Will the Voters Be Fooled?

"The settlement of the Land of Israel is the essence of Zionism. Without settlement, we will not fulfill Zionism. It's that simple."

(Yitzhak Shamir, Israeli Prime Minister)

Prime Minister Benjamin (Bibi) Netanyahu has finally returned for a visit to Gush Shiloh (the historical Shiloh bloc of communities) in Samaria after an extended absence, both physically and in policy. Not coincidentally, his last public visit to this region was before the last elections. Now that national elections are once again around the corner on March 17th, Bibi has returned in a demonstrative show of support, visiting the community of Eli yesterday as part of his campaign to attract support for his Likud party from the Jewish residents of the area.

Should we be excited at the prospect of a new Bibi and run to vote Likud?

Let's not forget that this is the same Bibi who has, throughout his term:

1.   ... continued to support an unofficial freeze on Jewish building in Samaria, while allowing the construction of a new Arab city in the heart of Samaria.

2.   ... refused to endorse the Levy Report, which he had commissioned, and which proves that Israel cannot legally be called an "occupier" of Judea and Samaria. This report, if approved by the next coalition, can lead to a Jewish building boom that will substantially change the facts on the ground.

3. ... continued to support the creation of a so-called Palestinian state, albeit demilitarized (Remember that same demand in Gaza?) in the biblical heartland of Israel.

Those who say "Vote Bibi" for fear of the Left getting elected should carefully watch the polls. The Likud has been consistently ahead of Labor and its so-called Zionist Union in most of the recent polls, so it seems clear that the Left will not win. However, if Likud is too powerful, Bibi will again empower his left flank and appoint left-leaning ministers to the Defense, Justice, and Foreign Ministries. The parties to the right of the Likud, such as Jewish Home, if strengthened in the upcoming elections, are the best guarantee that Netanyahu will not repeat the sad history of having the Likud, a right of center ruling party, carrying out left-wing policy. By voting for and buttressing the strength of those to the right of the Likud, the next Likud-led coalition will be pulled rightward, and will thus be more likely to implement policies that strengthen our hold on the Land of Israel.

Ya'alon Encourages Building Homes: For Arabs Only!

"Remember your servants Abraham, Isaac and Israel, to whom You Yourself swore 'I will give your descendants all this land I promised them and they will inherit it forever.' "

(Exodus 32:13)

According to the most recent pre-election surveys, the Likud has been rising and the Jewish Home has been falling. Unless this trend is reversed and the strength and subsequent clout of the Jewish Home party grows unexpectedly, it should be clear to all that Moshe Ya'alon (Likud) will once again be the Defense Minister of Israel in the next governing coalition.

As was evident in Ya'alon's weak, indecisive leadership in the most recent Gaza conflict, known as Operation Protective Edge, when he had to be urged by Minister of Economy Naftali Bennett (Jewish Home) to destroy the Hamas tunnels, such a scenario is very problematic for Israel's security. The Islamic terrorist leaders certainly won't be trembling in their boots at the prospect of another few years with Ya'alon at the helm.

The threats on Israel's southern and northern borders are very real and imminent, as is the Iranian nuclear threat. These serious challenges to the security of Israel require a firm, decisive hand that will clearly put the safety of Israel above all other concerns and won't fight another non-war of multiple ceasefires at the enemy's whim.

The problem, however, goes way beyond Ya'alon's weakness in leading the battlefield efforts. It was reported yesterday that he has been pulling out all the stops to further the infamous Rawabi project, building a new Arab city in the heart of Samaria. Despite his refusal, presumably with Prime Minister Netanyahu's tacit support, to approve new Jewish communities and/or building projects in both Samaria and Judea, Ya'alon has been doing everything in his power to facilitate the infrastructure work on Rawabi, expected to be an Arab city with 40,000 residents. Such a disproportionate project will badly choke the two neighboring Jewish communities of Halamish and Ateret, both of which have been suffering under Netanyahu and Ya'alon's unofficial freeze on the issuing of permits for Jewish building in Samaria.

As if that's not bad enough, Ya'alon's passion for the Palestinian cause is causing him to break all the rules to increase Arab settlement in Samaria. The Rawabi project has been temporarily stalled, mainly because of the lack of water infrastructure, which requires approval from the Israeli-Palestinian Joint Water Committee (JWC). This committee has not met for the last five years because of the Palestinian Authority's refusal to meet with Israel. Ya'alon has incredibly been trying to bypass the authority of Infrastructures Minister Silvan Shalom, who has rightly insisted on following proper procedure for this project.

As one who has shown a perverse passion for furthering Palestinian Authority interests in Samaria, Defense Minister Ya'alon is clearly not suited for his position. If Jewish Home doesn't succeed in increasing its Knesset representation on March 17th, thereby strengthening its bargaining power in coalition negotiations, we can expect Prime Minister Netanyahu to reappoint Ya'alon to his position. Such a move would be tragic for the cause of Jewish rebuilding in Judea, Samaria, and eastern Jerusalem, as well, all of which require the Defense Minister's approval. Ya'alon is not fit for the job.

Good Jobs for ISIS and Hamas

*"We cannot win this war by killing them. We need
... to go after the root causes that lead people to join
these (terror) groups, whether it's lack of opportunity
for jobs or ..."*

(US State Department Spokeswoman Marie Harf)

In the legendary American TV comedy, "I Love Lucy",
Lucy's husband Ricky frequently complained about
his wife's "hair-brained schemes", in which she tried
to accomplish her objectives in ever-so convoluted ways. Not
to be outdone by the effervescent, creative Lucy, the Deputy
Spokeswoman at the US State Department, Marie Harf has
come up with a novel approach for ending the scourge of
Islamic terrorism – Give them jobs!

In a series of interviews at major media outlets, Harf
reiterated her plan to defeat ISIS. In one such interview on
MSNBC, she declared, "We cannot win the war on terror,
nor can we win the war on ISIS, by killing them. We need to
find them jobs. We need to get to the root cause of terrorism
and that is poverty and lack of opportunity in the terrorist
community."

In other words, a good food stamps program, child-
support payments, college scholarships, and assistance in
obtaining a mortgage will end the mass beheadings of non-
Muslims.

Harf's solution would actually be quite amusing if it wasn't
coming from a top official in the Obama administration.
Furthermore, it exposes a serious lack of understanding of the
Muslim mentality and the ideology from which its dangerous
seeds germinate. The central precept of Jihad in Islam refers
to "holy war against the unbelievers." This deeply held belief,

which comes from the core of Islam, cannot be bought out by a new car or television.

Several prime examples of top Islamic terrorists who killed Americans and whose passion for killing "infidels" doesn't come from poverty:

- Osama bin Laden – the infamous founder and leader of Al Qaeda came from a wealthy Saudi Arabian family and was known to be worth somewhere between $50-300 million.

- Umar Farouk Abdulmutallab – The failed "underwear bomber" came from one of the wealthiest families in Nigeria, where his father was chairman of the First Bank of Nigeria.

- Ayman al-Zawahiri – the current leader of Al Qaeda, is a trained eye surgeon, certainly not a product of poverty.

- Mohammed Atta – the main organizer of the 9/11 attacks, came from a background of privilege. His father was a lawyer, educated in both sharia and civil law. His mother came from a wealthy farming and trading family and was also educated. Atta was a graduate student in Germany when he became radicalized.

This short list, of course, doesn't include the thousands of ISIS members that have been recruited from affluent Western countries, nor does it include the thousands of Hamas and Fatah terrorists who grew up under Israeli rule in Judea, Samaria and Jerusalem, enjoying a much higher standard of living than Muslims in every neighboring country.

The bottom line is that the State Department spokeswoman

revealed a shocking arrogance in her statements, ignoring the real motivation for Islamic terrorism. Most Muslims who join terrorist groups do so because they believe in what they have been taught is a higher cause and ideology, as repugnant as it may be to those in the free world. True, the perverse Islamic ideology endorses beheadings, sexual abuse of women, and the acquisition of wealth through terrorism, but the root cause is not poverty.

Islamic terrorism will only be defeated when the evil ideology at its core is recognized and attacked simultaneously at all levels – military, educational, and legal. Not through hair-brained schemes hatched by misguided Washington liberals.

Netanyahu's Churchill Moment

"Politicians all too often think about the next election. Statesmen think about the next generation."

(Linda Lingle, American politician)

Will Israeli Prime Minister Benjamin Netanyahu soon be walking in the footsteps of the great British statesman Winston Churchill? In less than twenty-four hours, Prime Minister Netanyahu will be delivering his much anticipated presentation about the nuclear threat from Iran to the joint houses of the United States Congress. This significant speech, controversial as it has become, will indeed be the speech of a lifetime for Netanyahu, with significant military and political ramifications on both sides of the ocean.

In recent days, the political darts have been flying fast and furious, and have been aimed at Netanyahu from three primary directions, each with a not-so-altruistic interest in minimizing the impact of his presentation:

- ***The Obama Administration*** – The pressure in the form of not-so-veiled attacks on Netanyahu has been intense from President Barack Obama through his surrogates, who are hoping that the imminent nuclear deal between the P5+1 powers and Iran will be the shining crown achievement of his second term in the White House. As the March 31 deadline for an agreement with Iran approaches, reports coming out of Jerusalem have made it clear that the proposed deal will enable Iran to gradually achieve nuclear weapons capability. Obama is concerned that Netanyahu's speech may actually succeed in exposing the danger to Israel and the free world, thus torpedoing the deal.

- **The Zionist Camp (Labor-HaTnuah) Political Party** – In fear of the boost that a powerful speech to Congress might give Netanyahu's Likud in the March 17 elections, the Israeli Left is having political conniptions over the Netanyahu speech. Despite the fact that Zionist Camp co-leader Herzog has stated that he shares Netanyahu's views on the Iran issue, he and his colleagues are vigorously stoking the political flames by publicly criticizing the speech, as well as Netanyahu's character.

- **The Iranian Regime** – Even though the Iranian leadership has been quoted as saying, "The Americans are begging for an agreement", the mullahs who control Iran are, in fact, quite eager for a deal that will enable their nuclear weapons program to go forward, albeit with some restrictions that will essentially only affect the timing of its implementation. Therefore, they are very concerned about the potential impact of the speech to Congress.

An Opportunity For Greatness

In summation, Congress can be very influential in approving or disapproving of the impending deal and that is where the Prime Minister's focus must be. Secretary of State John Kerry's announcement that he will be in Geneva negotiating with Iran during the Netanyahu speech speaks volumes about the Obama administration's general abandonment of one of America's closest allies.

Despite, or maybe because of this very public drama, all eyes will be on Washington tomorrow when Netanyahu delivers what promises to be the speech of a lifetime. The late and great British Prime Minister Winston Churchill was known for his powerful speeches warning the free world about the Nazi threat, as well as the need to stand up to the danger of Islam, even though the Muhammadan religion was then at a much earlier stage in its Jihadist actualization. For Netanyahu, in the age of almost nuclear Iran, ISIS, Hamas, and Hezbollah, this will truly be a Churchill moment, an opportunity to inspire the world to action, and indeed, to greatness. The message is much greater than the petty politics on both sides of the ocean, and hopefully, he will boldly rise to the occasion. Will his message be heeded?

One Week to Israeli Elections:
Who Will Be the Winner?

"Popularity should be no scale for the election of politicians. If it would depend on popularity, Donald Duck and The Muppets would take seats in the Senate."

(Orson Welles, American film producer, actor, director)

As we enter the final week of the Israel election campaign, everyone is wondering who will win the leadership battle between the two main parties, the right of center Likud and the left-wing Zionist Camp, but should that really be the main question?

In the latest polls, Prime Minister Benjamin (Bibi) Netanyahu's Likud appears to be running neck and neck with Yitzhak (Buji) Herzog and Tzipi Livni's joint party. However, in Israel's proportional election system, the party that wins the most votes doesn't automatically form the government. The prime example was in 2009, when one of Livni's previous parties, Kadima, won 28 seats in the Knesset to the Likud's 27, but she couldn't put together the necessary majority with the other parties in the 120 seat Knesset.

With the latest polls showing the race between the two main parties too close to call, the real question becomes the relative strength of the middle-sized parties such as Naftali Bennett's Bayit Yehudi (Jewish Home), Yair Lapid's Yesh Atid, and Moshe Kahlon's Kulanu, which are all currently estimated to receive between 8-13 seats. Another central question is what kinds of coalition deals will be formed in the days and weeks after the elections. One of the highlights of the previous elections was the unlikely post-election pact between Bayit Yehudi and Yesh Atid, which strengthened the post-election bargaining power of both. The eventual collapse of the Bennett-Lapid pact was, to a great extent, what led to the recent breakup of the governing coalition and to the upcoming March 17 election, as the right- left and religious-secular divide between those two medium-sized parties proved too great to pass the test of time. The subsequent infighting within the coalition then became unbearable as the unshackled Lapid moved to his more natural position on the left of the political spectrum.

Unless the Union of Arab parties, with its expected 12-14 seats, is invited into a possible Herzog-Livni coalition, the Left's prospects for gaining a Knesset majority are slim at best. Given a close election, that leaves Netanyahu as the likely head of the next coalition.

Assuming he is given that task, the real question is in which direction he will go in forming his new coalition. Netanyahu heads a party that often claims to believe in the complete Land of Israel, yet its leader publicly supports a demilitarized Arab "Palestinian" state in Judea and Samaria, a position that he reaffirmed this week. Furthermore, Likud believes in a free economy, yet its leader has been hesitant in confronting the major monopolies. The successful cell phone monopoly breakup, implemented by then Communications Minister Kahlon when he was still in the Likud, was a notable exception.

The respective electoral strengths of those middle-sized parties will determine the direction of the new coalition, as will the "day-after" deals which may give birth to new strategic partnerships. There were initially contacts between Lapid and Kahlon to form such a strategic partnership, although Kahlon's recent harsh criticism of Lapid's work as Finance Minister may have put a damper on those negotiations. Meanwhile, it has been reported that Bayit

Yehudi's Bennett is negotiating with Kulanu's Kahlon and separately with the Haredi (ultra-Orthodox) parties to explore such mutually beneficial arrangements for "the day after."

Yes, it will be interesting to see which of the two largest parties wins, but the actual direction of the new coalition may not be determined by Bibi, nor by Buji. Whatever the results on March 17, expect the coalition negotiations to last at least several weeks. If the election is close, Netanyahu will likely be tasked with forming the next government, after which he will probably use the threat of a Bibi-Buji-Tzipi unity coalition to keep all of his potential junior partners in their place and to lower their demands. Following through on that threat would, of course, contradict his explicit and repeatedly stated campaign pledge not to join coalition forces with the Left, but then again, after Election Day, anything goes, right?

A Right Coalition
In Bibi's Hands – If He Wants It

"Arranged marriages often work better than ones
born out of love."

*(Vince Cable, British Business Secretary, speaking after the
establishment of a new governing coalition)*

On Election Day in February of 2009, Benjamin (Bibi) Netanyahu's Likud didn't receive the most votes, but, after it became clear that Tzipi Livni's Kadima couldn't piece together a coalition, he was given the mandate to do so and he succeeded. The problem was that he then turned left, appointing Labor's Ehud Barak as his Defense Minister.

Four years later, he did it again, choosing Tzipi Livni as Justice Minister and chief negotiator with the Palestinian Authority.

The problem is that Netanyahu always talks a strong right-wing line before the elections. When it's campaign time, he eagerly climbs the hills of Samaria, plants trees and speaks out against concessions. After the elections, he sings the praises of land for peace and two-state solutions, sends Id El-Fitr greetings to Mahmoud Abbas of the Palestinian Terrorist Authority, and even quietly negotiates with Hamas.

At the moment, Netanyahu is in "hug and hit" mode. He claims to love the Jewish Home party of Naftali Bennett, but tells everyone not to vote for them. He caresses the national religious Jews who are the natural supporters of those to the right of Likud that have been faithful to the Land of Israel and instead implores them to vote for the party that implemented the division of the Land of Israel.

What happens in the week after the elections? Each of the party leaders visits President Ruby Rivlin to recommend who he or she would like to see form the next governing coalition of Israel. The one ultimately selected by President Rivlin doesn't have to be the leader of the party that won the most votes in the election. That may be an important consideration, but the main goal is to create a stable coalition that reflects the will of the people, and therefore, it is very possible, perhaps even probable, that Netanyahu's Likud can lose the battle (the election), but actually win the war (the coalition).

Labor's Yitzhak (Buji) Herzog (of the so-called Zionist Union with Tzipi Livni) can try to form a coalition with his natural partners on the left, the far-left Meretz and Yair Lapid's moderate-left Yesh Atid. The only other natural partner is the United Arab List, but they adamantly refuse to join a "Zionist" coalition, and furthermore, Buji would likely be reluctant to bring in such virulent haters of Israel. The Zionist Union, Meretz, and Yesh Atid may end up with a combined 40-42 mandates, far less than what is required.

To get to the minimum Knesset majority of 61, Herzog needs to turn to other parties, and therein lies the problem. Yisrael Beytenu leader Avigdor Liberman has repeatedly stressed that he will not sit with the extreme left Meretz, nor will Meretz sit with him. In addition, the Haredim (ultra-Orthodox parties UTJ and perhaps Shas) have vowed repeatedly not to sit in a coalition with Yesh Atid, which leaves Moshe Kahlon's Kulanu as the only additional party that is possibly prepared to join a Herzog coalition, leaving Herzog short of the needed Knesset majority. Yes, politicians often talk a different game after elections, but these particular vows are based on especially deep-rooted animosities and are likely to withstand the test of time and perhaps even financial incentive.

Netanyahu, on the other hand, can count on his natural

partners, Jewish Home and the Haredim, along with Eli Yishai's new Yachad party. Together, if the polls are correct, they will have approximately 50 seats between them. Add on Yisrael Beytenu and Kulanu and you have a fairly stable majority of about 65 mandates.

Therefore, those on the right need not excessively fear a coalition of the Left, but certainly, there is a need to be concerned about Netanyahu joining together with Herzog, since he has been prone to turn left after elections in the past.

For that reason, it is absolutely critical that everyone vote and bring many others along with them. Keep in mind that there are those who are in need of assistance to vote and that there are those who are prone to forget, and therefore, it's essential to be active in helping to get out the vote.

As long as the Israeli Right votes for the party that best represents its views, there will be a stable right-wing coalition formed by Netanyahu. That is, of course, assuming that he won't suddenly go left on March 18 to form a national disunity government with Herzog. The way to prevent that is by voting for the genuine right, so Netanyahu's natural partners will be so strong that it will be in his interest to form a genuinely right of center coalition.

Bibi's Sweet Revenge

"Revenge is sweet and not fattening."

(Alfred Hitchcock, British film director)

Jews don't believe in taking revenge, even if it is sometimes unavoidable. Nonetheless, if revenge is not the best word to describe what happened in Israel this week, there is at least a unique kind of sweet justice in Prime Minister Benjamin (Bibi) Netanyahu's electoral victory over the Left's Labor, which called itself the Zionist Union for the purposes of this election.

While there may be no hard proof uncovered yet, it has certainly been one of this campaign's most widely-known secrets that the elites of Israel's mainstream media formed an unofficial alliance with the Left's "Anyone but Bibi" campaign.

That aggressive and obviously well-funded political operation was run by the One Voice and V15 (Victory in 2015) organizations, the former of which was apparently financed by the US State Department to the tune of at least $250,000 and possibly much more. The dirty trail apparently leads all the way to the White House, as the director of V15 is none other than Jeremy Bird, who was President Barack Obama's National Field Director in 2012.

The continuing revelation of this blatant international interference, now being investigated by a US Senate committee, hit a raw nerve with the traditional Israeli public that was already upset about the Left's self-righteous verbal ridicule, at their political rally a few weeks ago of "those who kiss mezuzot" (the Torah parchments on Jewish doorposts). But the never-ending arrogance of the secular elites was ultimately destined not to go unanswered.

When this vicious campaign became known to all, especially as a result of the widespread publicity gained by the well-attended rally for the Land of Israel last week, there was a strong backlash, and the average Israeli spoke his mind at the voting booth on Election Day. Due to the polls predicting a Zionist Union victory, many voters who were planning to support the firmly right-wing religious Jewish Home party, altruistically shifted their votes to Netanyahu's Likud at the last minute in order to defeat the Left, but also perhaps as a direct response to the unbridled and unfair attacks on Netanyahu.

Netanyahu, who ran a powerful campaign, especially down the homestretch, can savor this moment of well-deserved victory. As for his nemesis in Washington, Obama and his administration will probably get what for them may be a nightmare, a right-of-center and religious coalition, headed by the man they love to hate.

Why The Jewish Home Needs Defense

"The only way to predict the future is to have power to shape the future."

(Eric Hoffer, American writer)

Yes, I know it's a play on words, but it's truer than ever, in either context.

Israeli Prime Minister Benjamin Netanyahu and his prospective coalition partners are in the midst of intense negotiations over the formation of the new governing coalition. Will he keep his promise to the voters that the religious Zionist (national-religious) Bayit Yehudi will be "a senior partner" in his coalition?

In the build-up to the elections, Netanyahu moved sharply rightward, visiting communities in Judea and Samaria, vowing to prevent the establishment of a Palestinian state, and repeatedly emphasizing that Bayit Yehudi will be the primary partner in his coalition, regardless of how many mandates it has in the Knesset.

This was all part of a blatant, targeted operation to get Bayit Yehudi voters to switch their votes to Netanyahu's Likud, thereby ensuring that he would solidly win the election, rather than his leftist opponent Yitzhak Herzog. The strategy worked, well beyond all expectations, and Likud won a big victory with 30 mandates (as opposed to an expected 20-23), while Bayit Yehudi plunged to 8 (as opposed to an expected 11-13).

The massive nationalist rally in Tel Aviv, held two days before the election, was a national-religious show of force. Organized by Daniella Weiss, one of the great pioneers of the Jewish settlement movement in Samaria, the participants were overwhelmingly from the national-religious public, natural Bayit Yehudi supporters. Netanyahu, given the lectern as the primary speaker, urged all of those present to show their nationalist credentials, only by voting Likud, thereby preventing the leftists from giving away the Land of Israel, specifically Judea, Samaria, and Jerusalem. He was followed by Bayit Yehudi leader Naftali Bennett, who played his guitar, praised the Land, People, and Torah of Israel, but didn't say a word about who to vote for.

The message received by the voters was clear – It's okay to vote for Likud – we have iron-clad promises that the national-religious will be the senior partner in the new coalition. Meanwhile, we have to save Netanyahu, and us, from a defeat at the hands of the Left.

The national-religious public followed through on that message, flocking en mass to the polls to vote Likud. The same public that experienced withdrawals, building freezes, and the release of terrorists under Netanyahu's leadership, proved to have a short memory. True, the intention of the national-religious who voted Likud was to prevent a leftist victory, which is in fact what happened, but in doing so, they may have greatly decreased their own influence in the new government that is about to be formed. Bayit Yehudi is now dependent on the fulfillment of Netanyahu's pre-election promises.

In this context, today's announcement of a new government-ordered freeze on building in the Har Homa neighborhood of Jerusalem is particularly disturbing. The previous Netanyahu governments were noted for their official and unofficial building freezes in eastern Jerusalem, as well as in Judea and Samaria. All construction in these areas requires the approval of the defense minister; while ultimately, the overall policy is determined by the prime minister himself. Defense Minister Moshe Ya'alon and Defense Minister

Ehud Barak before him authorized repeated building freezes, causing a serious shortage of Jewish housing to meet the demand for apartments in Israel's capital city.

So the real question is – Will Netanyahu's new coalition reflect a real rightward shift, or were his campaign statements all a bunch of lies expressed for electoral purposes, while a naive national-religious public swallowed it willingly?

Now that negotiations are in full gear, it is critical that the Bayit Yehudi party (Jewish Home) be given authority over the Defense Ministry. Housing Minister Uri Ariel of Bayit Yehudi made great efforts during his brief term in office to unfreeze Jewish building in Jerusalem, in Judea, and in Samaria, but his hands were tied. The unofficial freezes on Jewish building continued, while at the same time a new Arab city, called Rawabi, is being rapidly built, with great fanfare and effort on the part of Defense Minister Ya'alon, in the very heart of Samaria. Short of the prime ministership itself, there is no greater position of influence than the defense ministry in freezing or renewing the rebuilding process in Judea, Samaria, and Jerusalem.

Contrary to the expected backtracking statements from Likud officials, Netanyahu does, indeed, owe a serious debt to the national-religious public that sacrificed its personal interest, albeit perhaps naively, for what it was told was the greater nationalistic good. They relied on Netanyahu's promises. Now it's time for him to deliver.

Netanyahu and Ya'alon Are Funding Islamic Terrorism

"If you see a snake, just kill it – don't appoint a committee on snakes."

(Ross Perot, American businessman)

It was announced today that Prime Minister Benjamin Netanyahu and Defense Minister Moshe Ya'alon have resumed the transfer of millions of dollars in tax funds to the Palestinian Authority. The funds are being transferred despite the continuing open hostility of the Fatah-Hamas controlled PA towards Israel, as well as its continuing financing of terrorism.

The funds had been withheld from the PA since January, in retaliation for its moves to join the International Criminal Court (ICC) and due to its diplomatic war against Israel in many other international forums, all of which is a blatant violation of the Oslo "peace" accords. The PA behavior hasn't changed for the better, so why reverse Israeli policy?

Prime Minister Netanyahu said that given "the deteriorating situation in the Middle East it is necessary to act with responsibility ... alongside a determined struggle against extremism."

The obvious problem with the PM's statement as that the PA is as extreme as they come and becomes more extreme every day. Aside from perhaps Iran, there is no governmental or quasi-governmental body that has a longer history of aiding and abetting Islamic terrorism in Israel and beyond.

The PA has been financing terrorism for the past 15-20 years by giving direct payments to terrorists and their families. Unlike the Netanyahu-Ya'alon duo, they don't make imaginary distinctions between "moderate" and "radical" terrorists. The PA is an equal opportunity employer that pays all terrorists for blowing up buses, shooting babies, and setting off bombs in the middle of crowds of people. Hamas, Fatah, Islamic Jihad, Al Qaeda, and ISIS are all funded and honored as worthy recipients.

The Netanyahu-Ya'alon argument that "international considerations" require this strategic blunder is both morally and strategically unacceptable. The PM's reelection campaign was based on his presumed "strength" in standing up to unfair foreign pressure. Since his election success, the free-fall has been shocking, as each unjust critique from the White House has been followed by another pathetic concession from Jerusalem.

Handing over funds to the Palestinian Authority is equal to giving direct funds to terror. Netanyahu and Ya'alon are playing a cynical and hypocritical game that won't be wiped away by a hundred powerful speeches to Congress.

Time To Attack Iran

"If someone comes to kill you, get up early and kill him first."

(Talmud: Sanhedrin 72:1)

The recently-signed framework agreement between the P5+1 group of nations and Iran, currently being promoted by the Obama administration and its many Democratic lackeys in Congress, has greatly increased the likelihood of a massive Israeli preemptive strike on Iran's nuclear facilities.

Even though the American (and other) sanctions on Iran haven't officially been removed, the wall has already fallen, as the psychologically weakened and, as always, money-hungry international community rushes to engage the ayatollahs. Russia's Putin was the first and most notable, finalizing an agreement to ship his country's S-300 missile defense system to Iran. Australia soon followed, reaching an intelligence-sharing agreement with the Islamic state.

These ominous signs on the horizon are only the beginning of a dangerous process of capitulation to Iran, as the world quickly recognizes what is evident to almost everyone aside from US President Obama and his clueless Secretary of State John Kerry, that Iran is being given the international green light to become a nuclear nation. Therefore, the world wants to get into its good graces.

If Iran was seeking nuclear power for peaceful purposes, it would be quite different, but the third largest oil-exporting country has absolutely no need for nuclear energy, unless it truly aims to fulfill its often declared goal of destroying Israel and exporting its Islamic revolution around the world, the latter of which it is already doing.

An Israeli preemptive strike on Iran's many nuclear facilities will not be easy. It will require a massive lightning assault that will be denounced by virtually every nation, but the longer Israel waits, the inevitable, subsequent diplomatic onslaught will be that much greater. There is no choice. Even renewed and increased American sanctions, however praiseworthy, and however well-intended by their Congressional advocates, will not stop the death march of the ayatollahs.

The clock is rapidly ticking. Sadly, it must finally be understood that the military option is the only realistic one. In two weeks, the new Israeli governing coalition will be officially established and government policy will be set in place. Let the planning begin.

Jimmy Carter's Ignorance and/or Hatred of Israel

"Real knowledge is to know the extent of one's ignorance."

(Confucius, Chinese philosopher)

Former US President Jimmy Carter is back again in Israel, along with his "Committee of Elders", once again lashing out at Israel, after Prime Minister Netanyahu and President Rivlin's refusal to meet with him.

According to Carter, "The (Elders Group) stands for peace and human rights, and if human rights and peace are not on Netanyahu's agenda, I understand why he does not want to meet us."

Carter expressed his sadness that the "two state solution" and "land for peace" seem to be increasingly out of favor with Israel's elected leadership, while warmly praising the authoritarian, terrorist leadership of the Palestinian Authority. He called for an "end to occupation and settlement expansion," speaking, of course, about those "problematic Jews" who merely want to live in the historic biblical heartland of Israel.

What is the biblical heartland, you ask, Jimmy? Remember your beloved Bible? The Book of books that you once held dear as you were running for President the first time? It's the same Bible that talks about the regions of Samaria (north of Jerusalem) and Judea, (south of Jerusalem), the areas that you insist on calling by the fictional, non-historical, non-biblical term, the West Bank. Have you ever read about a place called the West Bank in your Bible, Jimmy?

If Carter was ignorant of both Bible and history, we could

certainly dialogue with him, but I can't believe that a former leader of the free world and a self-proclaimed Christian (not Catholic) can be so ignorant of his Bible, unless he believes in the ridiculous, albeit hateful Replacement Theology that claims that "the Church" has replaced the Jews as God's chosen people. As has become well known, much of the Christian world, led by North American Christians, is very supportive of Israel, but this "theology" of hatred, combined with ignorance, has been adopted by a lesser-known part of the Christian world as their religious justification for opposing the Jewish State.

Jimmy Carter, for all of his professed sincerity coupled with his infamous smile, is a charlatan, a hater of Israel, or a combination thereof. Prime Minister Netanyahu and President Rivlin were correct in not meeting with him, nor with his self-proclaimed "Committee of Elders".

Bennett Stand Strong!

"We hope the world will act in the spirit of enlightened self-interest."

(Atal Bihari Vajpayee, Indian statesman)

Bypassing the Jewish Home party, Prime Minister Benjamin Netanyahu's Likud has handed over the entire Religious Affairs Ministry, including full power over the religious courts, to the unrepentant former convict Aryeh Deri of the anti-Zionist Shas, effectively reversing the wise and prudent reforms in the conversion system, among others, that had been implemented by Rabbi Eli Ben-Dahan (Jewish Home).

With the deadline for the forming of a coalition looming, Netanyahu's sudden fait accompli has certainly presented Jewish Home leader Naftali Bennett with a very difficult dilemma. Should he suffice with just the Education Ministry and two lesser ministries, as has been offered by the Likud?

Rightly disturbed by Netanyahu's sudden capitulation to the corrupt Deri's demands, Bennett is now demanding the Justice Ministry for MK Ayelet Shaked as compensation. Likud honchos are warning Bennett that they won't agree to his new demand and that the Likud will instead invite the leftist "Zionist" Forum of Isaac Herzog and Tzipi Livni to join the coalition, thereby breaking another of Netanyahu's solemn campaign pledges, specifically that the Likud will not invite the leftists into the coalition. The Likud spokesman then went on to loudly declare that the "national religious public would never forgive Bennett" for allowing such a coalition to be formed.

I strongly disagree. The onus should be only on Netanyahu,

and Bennett should force his hand. After apparently lying to the national religious public repeatedly about his true intentions, Netanyahu doesn't deserve its support (nor did he deserve it on Election Day). Bennett should hold firm in his demands. If Netanyahu runs to the Left, it will be clear to all where his real loyalties lie. Clarification is critical, since there is no purpose in entering the Likud-led coalition if its leader, despite his repeated and very vocal campaign vow to form a strong right-wing government with Jewish Home in a "senior position", is instead looking for a coalition with an emboldened Left.

This is, indeed, a clarification test for Netanyahu. Who does he really want in his coalition?

Israel's New Government:
Three Women to Watch

"If you want something said, ask a man; if you want something done, ask a woman."

(Margaret Thatcher, British Prime Minister)

While the exaggerated emphasis on the physical appearance of female politicians around the world is absolutely unfair, and even sexist, the title of this article is merely a play on words, as it refers to the non-physical attributes of three very capable women in Prime Minister Netanyahu's new governing coalition. In this coalition, there are some new faces and some old ones, but who are the ones that we should watch closely as they take up their new ministerial posts?

The answer:

Tzipi Hotovely (Likud) – Deputy Foreign Minister

The PM refused to appoint a Foreign Minister, officially reserving the position for himself, with the thought of possibly appointing current opposition members Avigdor Liberman (Yisrael Beytenu) or Yitzhak Herzog (Zionist Union) to the position, thereby broadening his coalition. This may, however, be an unlikely scenario, and Netanyahu's desire not to fill the position may, in reality, be partially due to his fear of emboldening future political rivals within the Likud, such as Gilad Erdan, Yisrael Katz, or Silvan Shalom. In any event, the lack of a full-time Foreign Minister certainly empowers the appointed Deputy Foreign Minister, Tzipi Hotovely, a religious, right-wing MK, who is a firm proponent of Jewish sovereignty in Judea and Samaria (the so-called West Bank).

Hotovely has never hidden her opinions and can be expected to share them with the many world leaders and media figures whom she is certain to meet.

Miri Regev (Likud) – Minister of Culture and Sport

The appointment of the outspoken Regev is already causing violent conniptions in the bodies of the leftist elites that dominate Israeli culture and entertainment. Asked for her opinion of the Regev appointment, singer Ahinoam Nini responded, "Miri Regev as Culture Minister? I don't believe it. Shock and amazement." Performer Shayke Levy told the Walla media site: "How do I feel about the appointment? I am out of feelings. I am empty of feelings. I don't know where it is leading us. I really don't know where it is leading. It seems the world is about to be destroyed. It must be the end of the world, so they are distributing the loot and that's all. I think it's a loss of direction." Such bombastic statements would indicate that some of the official left-wing biases in the world of state-supported culture may be tempered by the new minister, who seems determined to take her job quite seriously and is unlikely to be easily intimidated.

Ayelet Shaked (Jewish Home) – Justice Minister

As an activist MK, Shaked often voiced her disapproval at the self-selecting Supreme Court system and the secular-left biases of the legal system as a whole. Add to this the problem of a string of attorney-generals who have stymied the efforts of the people of Israel, and occasionally their government, to provide security to the nation and to exercise their rights to live in all parts of the Land of Israel currently in our possession. Expect the no-nonsense Minister Shaked to confront these challenges using all of the powers granted to her office.

The three competent women described above can each

be expected to spare no effort in attempting to shake up the system, by ceasing to accept the old, failed and tired mantras of land for peace, judicial activism, and the "legitimate rights" of the so-called Palestinians. A proud Israeli narrative would be a novel change from the accepted norms, as provided by the left-wing secular elites of Israeli society. Will the PM allow his new ministers the autonomy to be proactive on behalf of Israel?

Kudos to Hotovely: Yes, This Land is Our Land!

"The Lord said to Abram, Go out from your country, from your homeland and your father's house to the land I will show you."

(Genesis 12:1)

Since Prime Minister Benjamin Netanyahu hasn't yet named a Foreign Minister in his new government, Deputy Foreign Minister Tzipi Hotovely is currently serving in that capacity, and she's not wasting any time in changing the language of Israeli diplomacy.

In her first speech to Foreign Ministry employees in Israel and around the world, Hotovely declared, "Many times it seems that in our international relations, more than emphasizing the rightness of our cause, we are asked to use arguments that play well diplomatically, but at a time when the very existence of Israel is being called into question, it is important to be right."

She then gave a concrete, more personal example to illustrate her point that the justice of Israel's cause is the real issue: "If I wear your coat because I'm cold, and I can prove pragmatically and analytically that it really is cold for me, the world will ask a primitive and analytic question: Who does the coat belong to? In this context, it is important to say that this coat is ours, this country is ours, all of it. We didn't come here to apologize for that."

Hotovely then went on to cite Rashi, the biblical commentator, who, in his famous commentary on the first verse of Genesis states that the reason the Torah began with the story of creation, was so that when the world would call

Israel robbers for having stolen the Land of Israel from others, the Jews would be able to answer that the land belongs to God, and that He gave it to whom He desired.

Yes, we have returned home to our God-given eternal homeland, the Land of Israel, where we were a sovereign nation far longer than the combined age of the United States, Canada, and Mexico. There is no reason to apologize for this, especially when we are confronted with the regional Muslims who call themselves Palestinians, borrowing the fictional term that the Roman invaders used nearly 2,000 years ago when they exiled Israel from its land. Given that the Hebrew root of their adopted name means a robber, an invader, or one who takes something that doesn't belong to him, the relevance of that biblical commentary in our times becomes ever so clear.

Hotovely is off to a great start, as she attempts to change the rules and the language of the diplomatic game. Wishing her much success and hoping that the PM will adopt her positive approach. The complexities of diplomacy often demand simplicity and clarity. May it continue!

Radical Islam and the Invisible Feminists

"He (the rapist) showed me a letter and said, 'This shows that any captured women will become Muslim if ten ISIS fighters rape her.' There was a flag of ISIS and a picture of Abu Bakr Al Baghdadi."

(22-year-old non-Muslim rape victim; raped by 11 ISIS fighters)

I rarely use the term "Radical Islam", even though it seems to be the term favored by most of the world to describe the Jihadist oppression and abuse of women and children, as carried out in much of the Islamic world. I think it far more accurate to describe the danger of the Jihadist, oppressive philosophy that lies at the core of Islam, and which is certainly radical.

However, it is true that are varying levels of intensity and levels of abuse of women and children in the Islamic world, but any objective observer has to wonder where the liberal feminists are on this issue. Indeed, why are they in hiding? Where is their outrage about the abuse of women in the Islamic world, which far outflanks anything that occurs in the West?

Verbatim from the Washington Post (May 22, 2015):
Zainab Bangura, the UN's special representative on sexual violence in conflict, recently conducted a tour of refugee camps in the shadow of the conflicts in Syria and Iraq, war-ravaged countries where the Islamic State commands swaths of territory. She heard a host of horror stories from victims and their families and recounted them in an interview earlier this week with the Middle East Eye, an independent regional

news site.

> "They are institutionalizing sexual violence," Bangura said of the Islamic State. "The brutalization of women and girls is central to their ideology."

Bangura detailed the processes by which "pretty virgins" captured by the Jihadists were bought and sold at auctions. Here's a chilling excerpt:

> After attacking a village, (the Islamic State) splits women from men and executes boys and men aged 14 and over. The women and mothers are separated; girls are stripped naked, tested for virginity and examined for breast size and prettiness. The youngest, and those considered the prettiest virgins fetch higher prices and are sent to Raqqa, the IS stronghold.
>
> There is a hierarchy: sheikhs get first choice, then emirs, then fighters. They often take three or four girls each and keep them for a month or so, until they grow tired of a girl, when she goes back to market. At slave auctions, buyers haggle fiercely, driving down prices by disparaging girls as flat-chested or unattractive.
>
> We heard about one girl who was traded 22 times, and another, who had escaped, told us that the sheikh who had captured her wrote his name on the back of her hand to show that she was his "property."

Estimates vary, but there are believed to be somewhere between 3,000 and 5,000 women enslaved by the Islamic State. Many are Yazidis, a persecuted minority sect that the extremist Islamic State considers to be apostate "devil-worshippers," in part because of the Yazidis' ancient connection to the region's pre-Islamic past. The Jihadists' treatment of Yazidi women, in particular, has been marked out by its contempt and savagery.

The West has seen the notorious beheadings, but the above report about the abuse of women and children illustrates, perhaps more than anything else, the vast mentality gap between the West and its Islamic terrorist enemies. To Israelis, it may be less of a surprise, as this is what we have seen Muslim radicals carrying out in the Middle East since the days of Muhammad, the founder of Islam who had 31 wives and unlimited sex slaves, some of whom weren't even physically mature.

Terrorism and sexual abuse, including the abuse of children, doesn't occur in a vacuum. It has a specifically Islamic context and justification. If Saudi Arabia and Jordan, and even Egypt, are surprised by the rise of ISIS, they shouldn't be. Yes, the violent acts of ISIS are shocking, but unless it's understood that these acts arise from the broader, Islamic historical and societal context, it won't be confronted properly – and that's why the West has failed miserably. ISIS is simply a wildly popular, albeit the most extreme manifestation of Muslims imitating Muhammad, who is known as "the Sunna" or the example to be followed by all Muslims.

Given the horrible abuse of women that was so graphically described above and that is spreading wildly in the Islamic world, when can we expect that the Left and the vocal feminists in the West will raise their voices in protest?

Will we hear from Hillary Clinton?

Will we hear from Oprah Winfrey?

Buji Blames Bibi (and Excuses Obama)

"I think President Obama views Israel as a problem that needs to be solved."

(Elliot Abrams, foreign policy adviser for US presidents)

US President Barack Obama's interview Tuesday on Israel's Channel 2, in which he pointedly threatened to stop defending Israel at the UN if the peace process isn't renewed, has greatly upset Labor party leader Yitzhak (Buji) Herzog. Did he respond by criticizing the American leader for abandoning Israel on the diplomatic playing field? Did he place the blame where it belongs – squarely on the shoulders of Palestinian Authority ruler Mahmoud Abbas for refusing to negotiate with the Jewish state?

Well, not exactly. Actually, Herzog lashed out at Prime Minister Binyamin Netanyahu, strangely accusing him of "humiliating" Obama and causing a crisis in US-Israel relations.

One has to wonder what the esteemed leader of Israel's Left thinks has caused President Obama's hostility towards Israel. Could it possibly be that such animosity was evident long before his very first confrontation with Netanyahu?

Let's examine a few relevant contributing factors:

1. Barack Hussein Obama had a Muslim father, who died when Obama was an infant, but whom he idolized, as evidenced in his book, "Dreams From My Father."

2. Obama was subsequently raised as a Muslim in Indonesia by his Communist mother and his Muslim stepfather.

3. Supposedly converting to Christianity, Obama spent twenty years as a devoted congregant in the church of Pastor Jeremiah Wright, who was known for his fiery anti-Semitic, anti-Israel, and anti-American sermons.

4. Obama's higher education and political career were launched with the help of American Black Muslim radical businessman Khalid al-Mansour, whose close ties to the Saudi royal family were well known. Such assistance was similarly provided by unrepentant American terrorist William Ayers.

5. Furthermore, Obama had a very close relationship with the virulently anti-Zionist Palestinian-American activist, Rashid Khalidi, in Chicago.

By the time he was elected President in 2008, Barack Obama's hostility to Israel was already a well-established integral part of his world-view, long before his first meeting with Benjamin Netanyahu, and that is why Herzog is way off base in accusing his PM of ruining Israel's relationship with its friends across the ocean. The proverbial Obama-Netanyahu trains were headed for a collision years before their first White House crash in 2009.

Herzog should consider educating himself about the real Barack Hussein Obama before playing petty politics with truth.

European Aggression: Time to Fight Fire with Fire

"There is no difference whatever between anti-Semitism and the denial of Israel's statehood. Classical anti-Semitism denies the equal right of Jews as citizens within society. Anti-Zionism denies the equal rights of the Jewish people its lawful sovereignty within the community of nations. The common principle in the two cases is discrimination."

(Abba Eban, Israeli statesman and diplomat)

With all the talk of BDS, coupled with the worldwide upsurge in anti-Semitism and bias against Israel, we are now being confronted with outright lies from official bodies in the European Union countries.

Fact:
Any Jew who travels in the so-called West Bank regions, which should always be called by their proper historical names, Samaria (north of Jerusalem) and Judea (south of Jerusalem), knows that Jews travel with doors locked and windows closed tight or protected, out of concern from the frequent Arab rock and firebomb attacks, not to mention actual shooting attacks. Knowing that Jews do not share their strange passion for attacking cars in transit, Arabs invariably travel in cars with windows wide open. Furthermore, they are often seen happily strolling on the sides of the main intercity roads, whereas Jews are forced to confine their walks to within their communities.

The Jewish safety precautions didn't arise in a vacuum.

The past fifteen years have seen thousands of Arab shootings, along with rock and firebomb attacks on Jewish civilians in Judea and Samaria, causing countless deaths and serious wounds, and many lifelong psychological traumas to children and families.

Meanwhile, the arrogant, self-righteous countries of Western Europe continue to officially disseminate incredible lies that rival the infamous Nazi and Soviet Communist propaganda machines in their viciousness and hatred of truth.

Travel Advisory – British Government Website:
"Israelis living in the illegal settlements in the West Bank occasionally organize demonstrations in the West Bank which sometimes turn violent. Take particular care if you are near any of these settlements..."

Travel Advisory – Dutch Government Website:
"There are security risks for traveling all over the West Bank including east Jerusalem. Be alert when traveling there. Demonstrations and violent incidents occur regularly. Jewish colonists live in illegal West Bank settlements and organize demonstrations regularly around and on the road. These colonists are sometimes violent. At times, these colonists throw stones at Palestinians and international vehicles, so be alert when traveling around settlements of Jewish colonists."

Jewish colonists? Are they serious? We are proud residents at home in our biblical, historical heartland, with generations and roots tracing back thousands of years, even though our Arab Muslim neighbors try to kill us every time we dare to travel outside our residential communities. I guess the former colonizing countries of Europe, who invaded and controlled countries that weren't theirs, never treated their propensity for "Projection", the unintentional psychological defense mechanism, through which one projects his own faults and shortcomings on others. Anyone who has traveled here in the region of Samaria, where I have lived for twenty-three years, knows that these European government websites contain outright lies that bear no remote semblance of truth.

The time has come to play hardball in opposition to the haters that claim to be our friends. Israel's political leadership should put an end to its nimble diplomatic dance in response to diplomatic aggression. No more gentle diplomatic consultations, no more mild requests for clarifications. Stop welcoming the Dutch and British diplomats as honored guests in Jerusalem until the malicious lies are removed from their official government websites. It's not pleasant, but it's time to fight fire with fire.

Spiritual Backbone Needed

"See, I have given you this land. Go in and take possession of the land that the Lord swore He would give to your fathers – to Abraham, Isaac and Jacob – and to their descendants after them."

(Deuteronomy 1:8)

The Minister of Foreign Affairs of the Czech Republic, Lubomir Zaoralek, from a nation relatively sympathetic to Israel's plight, has now added his name to the long list of foreign officials obediently chanting the already monotonous Palestinian State Mantra in the presence of Prime Minister Benjamin Netanyahu.

With each successive visiting official, one can see the effect of the pressure on both Netanyahu and his Defense Minister Moshe Ya'alon, with each departing plane leaving behind another Israeli concession, much to its enemies' delight. Just twenty-four hours after a rocket launched from Hamas-controlled Gaza landed in the city of Ashkelon, causing Ya'alon to order a preventative blockade on Gaza, the blockade has been speedily lifted. This will enable the renewed flow of construction materials, including cement, into the southern coastal region, thereby expediting the rebuilding of the terror tunnels.

For those who have short memories or didn't read the news last July, it's worthwhile to remember that those tunnels constructed by the Hamas Islamic terrorist organization were used for the purpose of smuggling weapons into and throughout Gaza and secretly transporting their terrorists into Israel. Some tunnels were destroyed in last summer's war, but many others were left intact. Meanwhile, the persistent reports of tunnel construction noise heard underneath the homes in Israeli communities that border Gaza should lead to a firm strengthening, not a weakening of the blockade. Why allow them to transport the cement and other materials, which they are using for tunnel construction in order to kill us?

The pattern of concessions under foreign pressure has continued for far too long. We know that this is our land historically and politically, but it's not only the Balfour Declaration of 1917 and the approval of the League of Nations that makes our cause correct. Our political leadership needs to acquire the spiritual, biblical backbone that comes from knowing this land was given to us by the Almighty and that we need not fear the threats of the nations as they continue to chant their robotic mantras of land for peace and the two-state solution.

As for Gaza, the message should be sent loud and clear to Hamas and their terrorist cohorts: Not one cement truck will be allowed into Gaza until every terror tunnel is destroyed. The same message should be delivered to every visiting foreign official. Most importantly, Israel's political leadership must remember the biblical imperative: Be strong, be courageous, and the God of Israel will stand with you!

Born in Jerusalem? Where's That?

"So there was great joy throughout Jerusalem, because nothing had happened like this in Jerusalem since the days of David's son Solomon, King of Israel."

(2 Chronicles 30:26)

By a 6-3 majority, the US Supreme Court has invalidated a law of Congress from 2002 that would have forced the State Department to alter its long-standing policy of not listing Israel on passports as the birthplace for Jerusalem-born Americans, instead listing only "Jerusalem." The court ruled that Congress "overstepped its bounds" with its action, which interfered with the executive branch's decision-making power on foreign policy.

American citizens born in Paris have it registered on their passports that they were born in Paris, France. Those born in Cairo are listed as having been born in Cairo, Egypt. Even those who were born in Havana have it registered that they were born in Havana, Cuba. Only Israel has an inferior status. The result of the Supreme Court ruling for American citizens born in Jerusalem is that they will continue to have their place of birth registered as Jerusalem, seemingly an island in space that has no country.

While the constitutional issues between the relative authority of the executive and legislative branches in the United States government are very real, the Supreme Court has, in effect, sided with those who refuse to recognize Jerusalem as Israel's capital, or even as part of Israel. Therefore, even if their intention was to emphasize the authority of the President to conduct foreign policy, the result of their decision is blatantly political and emboldens every nation and terrorist organization that refuses to recognize Israel's right to exist. And that, I believe, runs contrary to the will of the American people.

Paradoxically, the Supreme Court decision strengthening President Obama's authority on foreign policy issues will also be passed along to his successor, and therefore, we can expect Jerusalem to be a hot issue in the upcoming 2016 election campaign. Every candidate will have to take a stand on recognizing Jerusalem as Israel's capital and moving the American Embassy to the Israeli equivalent of Washington, DC or Paris or London.

But promises on this issue have been made by candidates before, only to be broken later. Just ask former President George W. Bush.

Will the next American president truly stand with Israel and its eternal capital?

Silencing Art?

"Forced funding of the arts – in whatever trivial amounts and indirect ways – implicates citizens in culture they might openly despise or blissfully ignore."

(Nick Gillespie, American journalist)

Leftist artists in Israel have been visibly furious this week over what they are calling a threat to free speech, in response to promises by Culture Minister Miri Regev and Education Minister Naftali Bennett to cut off funding for anti-Israel theater productions.

Artists from the film, theater, dance, literature and music industries published a letter Sunday, "protesting the non-democratic measures taken by the Education and Culture Ministries against artists whose creative works or outlooks do not jive with the prevailing spirit in these offices."

So they say, but is the halting of government funding for works of art that support anti-Israel boycotts (BDS) or that glorify Islamic terrorism really non-democratic? Can it honestly be called "silencing creators who don't align with the regime's position," as one left-wing Knesset member recently called it?

In a free society, we are obliged to allow artistic expression of all kinds, as long as it doesn't cause a direct and immediate danger to public safety. However, the tax-paying citizens are not required to fund all such expressions. In fact, it is the absolute opposite of democracy for the citizens of a free country to be forced to provide funding to every artistic program that runs blatantly counter to the values, indeed the very survival, of that country. Such government coercion in the form of such forced financing would be the antithesis of freedom, cynically carried out in the name of freedom.

The government elected by the people has an obligation to allow free speech and free expression, not to give government handouts to anti-Israel theater groups and other similar artists. Such groups have no moral or legal right to pick the pockets of the Israeli public, and therefore, the government ministers are correct in signaling an end to such theft.

Here We Go Again: Presidents and the Religion of Peace

"The precept of the Koran is, perpetual war against all who deny that Muhammad is the prophet of God. The vanquished may purchase their lives, by the payment of tribute; the victorious may be appeased by a false and delusive promise of peace ... but the command to propagate the Muslim creed by the sword is always obligatory, when it can be made effective."

(John Quincy Adams, American President)

Some world leaders have been known to have strange slips of the tongue, otherwise known as nonsensical babble based on wishful thinking, especially when speaking about Islam, commonly referred to as one of the three great monotheistic religions.

After September 11, 2001, when Islamic terrorists launched four terrorist attacks in one day, murdering over 3,000 Americans, most of them at the World Trade Center in New York City, then US President George W. Bush strangely proclaimed, "The face of terror is not the true faith of Islam. That's not what Islam is all about. Islam is peace."

While serving in an admittedly ceremonial post, Israel's current President Reuven Rivlin seems determined to speak the same mushy pie-in-the-sky rubbish as GW.

Speaking yesterday at the Jordanian Embassy in Tel Aviv, President Rivlin declared, "I grew up learning about the rich world of Islam that is full of beauty, kindness, and mercy."

How I wish it were so. If only Islam didn't follow the example of Muhammad, its founder, who proudly boasted about his strong leadership in beheading 900 Jews in one day.

Yes, the same Muhammad who forced his sexual will on 31 wives, unlimited concubines, and countless young girls. In the Muslim world, he is considered to be "the Sunna", the example to be followed by all Muslims.

If only Muslims didn't follow the Koran, which repeatedly calls for Jihad, or holy war against non-Muslims. Is it a mere coincidence of nature that virtually every terrorist organization today is Islamic? ISIS, Al Qaeda, Hamas, Hezbollah, Boko Haram, Fatah, and all of the other terrorist organizations base their beheadings, mass rapes, bus bombings, sniper attacks on civilians, and other horrible behavior on the teachings of Muhammad, which are the basis for Islam.

How I wish that Presidents Bush and Rivlin were correct, but the evidence speaks volumes and facts don't lie. Whatever the beauty, kindness, mercy, and peace that they claimed to have seen in Islam, it has long ago been overshadowed and trivialized by the pain of the victims of its passion for Jihad, along with its terrible abuse of women and children.

Sadly, that is the true face of Islam and it needs to be confronted, not pandered to with false platitudes from misguided world leaders.

This Time Oren Is Right

"They (Palestinians) endure the daily humiliations –
large and small – that come with (Israeli) occupation.
So let there be no doubt: the situation for the
Palestinian people is intolerable. America will not turn
our backs on the legitimate Palestinian aspiration for
dignity, opportunity, and a state of their own."

(Barack Obama, American President)

After leaving the ambassadorship in Washington, DC, Michael Oren (now an MK in the Kulanu party) unofficially began his political career by promoting a plan for unilateral Israeli withdrawal from the mountains of Judea and Samaria. This suicidal proposal has been thankfully ignored by the recently elected government, of which Oren's party is now an integral part. When that "land for terror" proposal was foolishly suggested about two years ago, I was quick to criticize the historian's failure to learn from history, referring, of course, to Israel's disastrous unilateral withdrawal from Gaza in 2005, which predictably brought war and terrorism to new heights, from Hamas-controlled Gaza to the cities of Israel.

For that reason, I was pleasantly surprised to read about Oren's recent and very candid recollections and analysis of his time in Washington, DC, as Israeli Ambassador. He shocked the Obama administration and indeed, many Knesset members, with his "revelation" that President Barack Obama has intentionally and methodically shifted America's foreign relations away from Israel and towards the Islamic world. Furthermore, in a Foreign Policy essay entitled "How Obama Opened His Heart to the Muslim World", Oren asserts that Obama's obsession with the Muslim world stems from the

Islam-practicing father who abandoned him, as well as the political worldview that he held long before he entered the White House.

While it's true that I already had written extensively about Obama's family and political background in my book, "The Islamic Tsunami: Israel and America in the Age of Obama", the very fact that these disturbing truths are now being written about and confirmed by Mr. Oren is commendable. Ambassadors and politicians tend to fear direct expressions of truth, for they are trained to think first about which world leader might be offended. While certainly understandable, this tendency to always play it safe, so as not to offend, often appears to both our allies and our enemies as deceptive or hypocritical.

While we Israelis are very respectful of the positive historical relationship that we have had with the United States as a country, there is no need to pussyfoot around issues or to lie about the genuine hostility that we have experienced from this White House, both in words and in actions. By very publicly revealing some of that truth, Oren has brought a refreshing candor to our international political discourse, in which honest expression often seems to be permitted for all, except Israel. Let's hope that the candor will lead to positive steps from the White House to prove that the Israeli perceptions are mistaken.

"ISIS Palestine": The Authentic Expression of Jihad

"I will cast terror into the hearts of those who disbelieve. Therefore strike off their heads and strike off every fingertip of them."

(Koran 8:12)

The ISIS organization has shocked pundits left and right, as well as ordinary folks troubled by what appear to be extreme expressions of what has come to be known in the free world as "Radical Islam" or "Islamism."

In the Koran, the so-called holy book of Islam, based on the teachings of its founder Muhammad, "Jihad" is repeatedly referred to in the context of holy war against all non-Muslims. Hence, there is no "Radical Islam" or "Islamism." There is only Islam, and the highest precept in Islam is its Jihadist philosophy, which is at its core, and which is the epitome of intolerance.

Therefore, we should not be surprised by the recent distribution of a flyer throughout eastern Jerusalem, in what is thought to be the first ISIS announcement in the Israeli capital. The flyer threatens Christians in the area with "revenge," and is signed by the organization "ISIS Palestine," as reported on Israel's Channel 10.

Revenge for what, you might ask? Certainly not for anything that has happened in the last few centuries. ISIS, Al Qaeda, Boko Haram, Hezbollah, Hamas, and other Islamic terrorist groups are attempting to carry to fruition what Muhammad preached and what he practiced.

That is the basis for terrorism, not only against Jews, but

also against all those who don't agree to submit to Islam. The modern version of Jihadist philosophy is still living in the turbulence of the Muslim-Christian wars dating back hundreds of years:

> "Allah's Apostle said: I have been ordered to fight with the people till they say, 'None has the right to be worshipped but Allah'."
>
> *(Hadith 4:196, Narrated Abu Huraira)*

> "Believers, if you yield to the infidels they will drag you back to unbelief and you will return headlong to perdition. We will put terror into the hearts of the unbelievers... The fire shall be their home."
>
> *(Koran 3: 149-151)*

ISIS is the actualization of the Jihadist philosophy that guides the Islamic terrorist organizations. While the currently dominant terrorist organizations in Israel, such as Hamas and Fatah will feel somewhat threatened by the "in your face" style of ISIS, the new kid on the block will continue to grow in numbers, because they will be seen as "the real deal." They are the authentic expression of no-holds-barred Jihad, whether in "Palestine" or elsewhere.

The beheadings carried out in Iraq, in France, in the UK, and elsewhere will only increase with time. Just as Muhammad bragged about beheading 900 Jews in one day, the Muslim world will continue to imitate "the prophet" by supporting ISIS and its future offshoots.

Nonetheless, even if Israel as God's chosen people and land is the immediate target, the end goal is total world domination. The folks in the West may eventually wake up, but unless it happens soon, it will be too late. The Islamic tsunami is gradually engulfing the West and the tide will not be easily halted.

Ya'alon on Marriage:
Defending Israel's Values?

"Europe, which gave us the idea of same-sex marriage, is a dying society, with birthrates 50 percent below replacement."

(Maggie Gallagher, American writer)

After the landmark decision by the United States Supreme Court granted the legal stamp of approval to homosexual marriage, Israeli Defense Minister Moshe Ya'alon (Likud) weighed in on the issue of public recognition and authorization of same-sex marriage. In an unexpected public announcement, Ya'alon expressed his personal approval, stating, "I hope countries, including Israel, will follow in the footsteps of the United States and grant this basic right to all."

While it wasn't quite clear why a defense minister needed to speak out on such a social issue, it did raise the question of how Israel will relate to the monumental decision, which most Americans on both sides of the issue would agree was akin to a social earthquake.

By a razor-thin 5-4 majority, the US Supreme Court had just ruled that the US Constitution guarantees a right to same-sex marriage. Since Israeli jurisprudence often follows American precedent, will Israel soon be moving in the same path when it comes to what has been proclaimed as "human rights for all", and will we soon follow this latest American legal revision of its values system?

In a free society, everyone has the right to live his personal life the way he wishes, as long as he's not hurting others. Sexual and intimate social issues are left to the individual bedroom and no one has the right to pry and interfere in what consenting adults choose to do. The difficulty lies in what the society publicly recognizes as being the societal norm. Every stable society throughout history has established standards for what it defines as the common good. No stealing, no polygamy, and no rape are obvious examples that are by no means the standard in all countries, but have been the recognized and legally-approved norm in Western civilization.

With the latest US Supreme Court decision, the traditional nuclear family, an institution central in the Judeo-Christian standards that have guided the United States since its inception, has been thrown to the wolves. What will be next? Relaxation of public nudity laws, perhaps? Legalized marriage between siblings, perhaps? Maybe even bestiality? When there is no moral compass for public behavior, things fall apart and no one knows where to draw the line. As a result of the now widespread 1960s philosophy of relative truth, a large portion of American society gradually abandoned the basic principles of the Bible, the system of morality that had been its general guide for over 200 years. The traditional family of husband, wife and children that had been the bedrock of the society soon began to collapse. Along with the new norm of birth out of wedlock, more and more Americans are foregoing traditional marriage. A recent study reported that 60% of households on the island of Manhattan are single person households.

So what will be the direction of our little Middle Eastern "light unto the nations"? Israel is a bit of an anomaly that often defies the trends in the Western world. Despite the loud and colorful LGBT parades that have become an annual ritual in Tel Aviv and Jerusalem in recent years, same-sex marriage is unlikely to be approved anytime soon, as marriage in Israel continues to be assertively traditional. Furthermore, periodic studies reveal a profound thirst for Jewish tradition and observance, even among supposedly secular Jews. A natural result of that trend is that, contrary to the patterns of reproductive behavior in the United States and Europe, the sizes of Jewish families are growing, along with the practice of Jewish religious ritual, and it's happening within traditional husband-wife-children families. Aside from the Torah's clear prohibition of homosexual relationships, the man-woman marriage relationship is clearly the basis for a positive Jewish family life throughout the Torah and its commentaries. Therefore, the current societal move in Israel towards tradition makes it highly unlikely that the established standard would go the other way.

Israel's activist and very liberal Supreme Court may seek to follow its American counterpart, but if it attempts to do so, it will be bucking the prevailing social trends in Israel, making it extremely unlikely that such a blatantly political move would succeed.

"Possible Terrorist Attack Attempt"???

"I have met guys who work the overnight shift at 7-11, selling Slurpees and Camels to insomniacs who have more introspection than a lot of people in the mainstream media."

(Bernard Goldberg, American journalist, and political commentator)

After the gruesome terror attack near Shiloh, the Jerusalem Post posted the following report:

"Shots were fired late Monday toward an Israeli vehicle traveling near the West Bank settlements of Shiloh and Shvut Rachel in **a possible terrorist attack attempt.** At least four people were initially reported injured, with three people sustaining serious wounds and one with light-to-moderate wounds. **Motives behind the incident were not yet clear.**" (Emphasis Mine)

As one who lives in Shiloh, which is centrally located in the mountains of Samaria, and who was wounded some years ago in a similar shooting attack along with my then three-year-old son, I am greatly disturbed by what I have just read on a news-site that I generally have respected. Of course, I am very distressed by this horrific terrorist attack, but I am even more shocked by how it is being reported. We have experienced so many shooting attacks in Samaria – many Israelis dead and many Israelis wounded and they are ALWAYS terrorist attacks with very clear motives – to kill or wound the Jews in the car and to frighten thousands of others.

Possible terrorist attack attempt? ... Motives not clear? I am grossly offended by this particular editor's awkward, or even worse, blatantly biased effort at ignoring an obvious attack, and a serious one at that by terrorists on a civilian car. Definitely Arabs. Definitely Muslims. Almost definitely Hamas, Fatah, or Islamic Jihad. Possibly even ISIS. Definitely not Jews. Definitely not common criminals. The Jerusalem Post should know better that the history of terror does indeed repeat itself every time and the ideological address is always the same.

As I am posting this blog entry, we don't yet know who the victims are, other than that all four, in their 20s, are suffering from bullet wounds to both upper and lower bodies. The military and political response by Israel should be rapid and strong, but the Jerusalem Post must issue a quick correction and an apology for this pathetic attempt at political "correctness" even if in the unconvincing guise of cautious reporting.

An Afterword (posted 22 hours later) – One of the wounded, Moshe Malachi Rosenfeld, has died of his wounds. The others are still being treated in hospital. The Jerusalem Post report has been slightly revised, implicitly admitting that it was indeed a terror attack, apparently directed by Hamas. They still are refusing to call the region by its accurate historical name "Samaria," preferring to use the Arab misnomer, "the West Bank."

The Best Response to Terrorism

"And all your children (Hebrew – *banayich*) will be students of God, and your children will have peace – Do not read this verse as 'children' (*banayich*), rather 'builders' (*bonayich*)."

(Talmud Brachot 64a)

After a string of terror attacks in the past week, which, as is often the case, disproportionately afflicted the residents of Samaria, the question must be asked – What is the government of Israel planning to do about it?

We remember well the visits of Prime Minister Benjamin Netanyahu before the 2015 elections, when he suddenly became Mr. Settlement, as he appealed for votes from the Religious Zionist public. However, elections pass quickly and so does a person's memory. The two separate terrorist murders that sent shockwaves through Samaria this week were in regions that have not benefitted from the very limited building that was allowed under the previous government in Judea and Samaria. Most of the building projects were in the few cities that are very close to the western edge of Samaria and Judea, while the many idealistic communities that have taken on the great challenge of settling the heartland of Israel were totally ignored.

Now is the time to put those campaign promises to the test. The best response to terrorism is building. For every terrorist attack in or near Shiloh, a new neighborhood in Shiloh! For every resident of Kochav HaShachar murdered, a new neighborhood in Kochav HaShachar!

That is how a proud people should respond to hatred – with love – love for the Land of Israel. Populating the Land of

Israel with the People of Israel is the most suitable expression of that love. Some may say that allowing building in our entire country shouldn't be only a response to terrorism. However, it is certainly a fitting response. The purpose of terrorism is to kill innocent civilians. The secondary purpose is to terrorize, hence, frighten us, so that we'll be afraid and run away. Our answer is that we will stay and grow and build for the future!

The next step is in the hands of our elected officials. Instead of complaining that their hands are tied, will they finally respond courageously, as true Israeli patriots?

Hillary Clinton: Better for Israel?

"A true friend never gets in your way unless you happen to be going down."

(Arnold H. Glasow, American author)

Hillary Clinton 2016 is undergoing an Israel re-branding process that she hopes will lead her back to the White House.

The seven years with President Barack Obama have been traumatic for Israel. The hostility towards Israel has extended from his passion for ending Israel's gradual rebuilding of its biblical heartland, including its eternal capital, Jerusalem, to his eager, no holds-barred rush to wrap up a nuclear deal with Iran, which is sworn to Israel's destruction. The deal, which reportedly is 99% completed, will, by most Israeli accounts, enable the Iranian ayatollahs to achieve full nuclear bomb capability within a short period of time. Therefore, the Israeli consensus position is that the deal to be concluded in the coming days will be disastrous for the Jewish state.

So where does Hillary stand on these two key issues and how they impact the relationship between our two nations?

At a Manhattan campaign fundraiser last week featuring a largely Jewish group of donors, Clinton defended Obama against charges he had weakened the US-Israel relationship, asserting that such criticism stemmed from a "perception" problem, according to a donor who was present.

At the same time, according to the Politico news site, she also suggested that if she were elected president she could correct that problem and bring the two nations closer.

"Diplomacy is all about personal relationships, and I've got my own relationships," she said, referencing her two-decade association with Israeli Prime Minister Benjamin Netanyahu.

Let's examine the substance of that relationship, as developed by Secretary Clinton during her term in office. Wherever they may fall in the political spectrum, Israelis will never forget Prime Minister Netanyahu's infamous trip to the United States during Obama's first term, when the President and his Secretary of State Hillary Clinton, in a huff over Israel's settlement policy, abruptly left Netanyahu and his advisers standing alone in the White House to fend for their own dinner. Most Israelis instinctively understood that the humiliation of Israel's leader in the eyes of the international media wasn't just a personal insult to Netanyahu, but was, in fact, an affront to Israel's national dignity.

So, too, Israelis remember similarly the visit of US Vice-President Joseph Biden to Israel during that same period. Near the start of Biden's visit, a municipal committee in Jerusalem, in a previously scheduled meeting, authorized the building of 900 apartments in Israel's capital. When she heard the news, Secretary Clinton was reportedly infuriated and she called Prime Minister Netanyahu, giving him a stern forty-five minute lecture (which the White House publicized afterwards) about the limits of Israel's sovereignty in its own capital city, the capital that the United States doesn't recognize to this day. This position is certainly ironic, given the fact that Israel's unified kingdom stood in Jerusalem far longer than the USA has even existed as a nation.

Concerning the Iranian nuclear threat, which is by all accounts an existential threat for Israel, Clinton has been speaking out of both sides of her mouth. According to Politico, several people who have heard her address the Iranian issue say the fact that different people can come away with such different interpretations is a testament to her nuanced approach to the issue and her skill as a politician, rather than any vacillation on the subject. "That's just smart politics," said one donor who supports the negotiations and recently talked to her about them. "Because, right now, you have the freedom to say all those things, so why would you commit and box yourself in until you saw what the deal was?"

Nonetheless, Israelis already know what the parameters are for this deal, if not the fine details, and it's undoubtedly a bad one for Israel. Even so, Clinton recently told another pro-deal donor that she was "very supportive of the negotiating process," the donor recalled, while a third funder said she boasted of her role in starting the talks. "So it seemed like she was supporting it," recalled the funder.

Bottom line – Hillary Clinton was a loyal anti-Israel soldier during her term as Secretary of State. Her position firmly opposing the rebuilding of Judea and Samaria and her pro-Iran deal position are quite consistent with the new Left initiative to gradually reorient America's relationship with Israel, in favor of the Islamic world. Americans who truly care about Israel should be wary of the latest Clinton "friend of Israel" offensive. Hillary the candidate can be expected to rely on the knee-jerk liberal sensitivities of American Jews, urging them to vote for her, while simultaneously wooing them to her side with pro-Israel platitudes that mean nothing.

Communist Mentality in the Rabbinate

"The human race divides politically into those who want people to be controlled and those who have no such desire."

(Robert Heinlein, American novelist and science fiction writer)

The recent Cabinet decision supporting the Shas-controlled Religious Affairs Ministry's demand to reject improvements to the rabbinical conversion system that had been previously approved by Rabbi Eli Ben Dahan (Jewish Home) was disappointing to all who want to see a more welcoming Chief Rabbinate.

Minister Ben Dahan's improvements to the system had been made with an eye to finally meeting the challenge of tens of thousands of Israelis who are not Jewish, according to the parameters in Jewish law. Many of these cases involve young adults who are children of Jewish fathers and non-Jewish mothers. Ben Dahan, in his role as Deputy Religious Affairs Minister in the last government, had enacted reforms aimed at streamlining the conversion process, which has long been criticized as being unduly bureaucratic, and certainly not "user-friendly," by allowing prospective converts to engage the process with Orthodox community rabbis outside their local municipality.

Freshman MK Bezalel Smotrich (Jewish Home-Tekuma) has taken a surprisingly closed-minded approach on the conversion issue, calling the decision to dump Ben Dahan's reforms "a positive and necessary one for the Jewish people," adding that "when we take away from the Rabbinate responsibility for the standards of conversion and allow various organizations and institutes to determine their own standards as they see fit, this will eventually lead to a situation where we can no longer be united. Even worse," he continued, "those whose conversions are not approved by the Rabbinate will not be accepted by large numbers of Jews, who would suspect the veracity of their conversion," pointing out another reason for his approval of the decision.

Smotrich's stand is disturbingly near-sighted in its flawed understanding of "unity" and of "the Rabbinate." The Chief Rabbinate, in its excessively centralized capacity, has failed miserably in solving one of the most serious social challenges facing the Jewish people today, effectively closing the door to halachic conversion. Just as in pure Communism, in which a lack of competition invariably leads to stagnation, the unwillingness of the Haredi-controlled Chief Rabbinate to decentralize and to delegate responsibility to a variety of Orthodox rabbis will freeze the process of making Judaism warm and welcoming to a sector of Israelis who have risked their lives for our nation. Indeed, many of those families had left the forced assimilation of the Soviet gulag hoping to be accepted in Israel as members of the Jewish people. It's indeed ironic that formerly Soviet Jews are being subjected to a strictly centralized, unwelcoming system that, in its structure, replicates and reminds them of the rigid, oppressive Communist system that they escaped from.

Smotrich's concern that "various organizations and institutes" would determine standards of conversion in a decentralized system is wholly unwarranted. What organizations is he referring to? Perhaps he's referring to the organization of Orthodox Tzohar rabbis that has worked tirelessly to reopen doors, according to halachic standards, to these lost Jews with love and kindness? Does he actually doubt the halachic integrity of Rabbi Ben Dahan and the many outstanding community rabbis who supported his efforts and many of whom would have been present on the local conversion courts?

The last thing that the Jewish Home party needs is a resident cheerleader for the renewed Haredi domination of the religious establishment, promoting a failed conversion system, a remnant of the worst intolerance and stagnation that, like it or not, is usually inherent in a heavily centralized system. Yes, the top usually loves absolute power and, sadly, that also includes some rabbis, but unity cannot and will not be achieved without simultaneously reaching out to all sectors of the Jewish population within the halachic system. If we continue in the present course, we will only increase intermarriage and alienation from Judaism in the Land of Israel. And that is the opposite of Jewish unity.

Five Reasons to Attack Iran

"You will not fear the terror of the night, nor the arrow that flies by day."

(Psalm 91:5)

As details of the agreement with Iran continue to emerge, it becomes more and more evident that the deal is an existential danger to the survival of the State of Israel. While it is seems clear that US President Barack Obama will be preparing a compensation package to placate Israel and other concerned nations in the Middle East, this will only increase the arms race in the region, thereby making nuclear conflict more likely, as the Persian Gulf nations will now feel compelled to achieve nuclear capability to counter the Iranian threat.

There is only one realistic way of stopping that nightmare scenario – an Israeli preemptive strike on Iran's nuclear facilities, with logistic support provided by Saudi Arabia and other Persian Gulf nations. Such support from concerned Sunni Muslim nations would be covert, but would provide a cushion to counter the expected international condemnation against any Israeli military offensive.

Sadly, there will be those Israelis who will warn against ruffling American feathers by launching an attack which would effectively scuttle the agreement, but such warnings should be ignored. The deal with Iran certainly cannot be relied on to protect Israel, and therefore, a preemptive action should be ordered ASAP for the following reasons:

1. There will be no surprise inspections of the Iranian nuclear facilities. Giving twenty-four days advance notice gives them sufficient time to hide the evidence of nuclear weapons production.

2.   The Parchin military plant and the Bushehr reactor, where substantial covert nuclear activity has taken place, are not even mentioned in the deal.

3.   The immediate removal of sanctions and the subsequent infusion of vast billions to Iran's coffers will lead to a sharp increase in Iran's already substantial support for Hamas, Hezbollah, and other terrorist organizations in the region.

4.   The longer Israel waits, the more complicated a preemptive strike will become, both politically and militarily.

5.   An early and effective lightning strike, while risky, will forestall a massive Middle East nuclear arms race.

If one is to believe the repeated claims of Israel's political leadership proclaiming that "Israel will know how to defend itself", there comes a time that bold action must be taken, despite the negative political reaction that is sure to come, at least publicly. However, the private praise for a successful operation will also pour in from every nation that has felt itself threatened by the madmen in Teheran.

Wishing Israel's political leadership the wisdom and especially, the courage to know how and when to do what is clearly necessary!

The Iran Deal:
Are American Jews Against Israel?

"The overlay here is a growing polarization between politically conservative and politically liberal Jews on many issues."

(Steven M. Cohen, American sociologist)

As the US Congress begins its sixty-day period of reviewing the Iran nuclear deal, American Jews are being tested as never before in their support for Israel. Will they raise their voices in opposition to an agreement that Israelis across the political spectrum are firmly against?

In the past, particularly on the contentious issues of Judea/Samaria and land for peace, those American Jews who stood vocally against Israel's elected center-right government could comfort themselves by pointing to the Israeli left, which has long supported the surrender of Israel's biblical heartland to the so-called Palestinians in exchange for the promise of peace.

On the issue of Iran, however, there is no such comfort, as Israeli opposition leader Isaac Herzog has called the Obama administration's Iran deal "a horrible deal, one that will go down as the tragedy of the ages."

Nonetheless, some American Jewish organizations are supporting the agreement and urging Congress to approve it. While firmly pro-Israel groups such as AIPAC are strongly opposing the agreement, the hard-left J Street organization has announced a multimillion-dollar national campaign to push forward the rather strange argument that the deal "advances both US and Israeli security interests" and "makes the United States, Israel and the entire world safer." Not missing a beat, the National Jewish Democratic Council, in announcing its "strong support" for the deal, concludes that it will "ultimately lead to a safer and more secure region."

Most Israelis and supporters of Israel would find such blatant falsehoods, which I would prefer to believe are based on ignorance, to be shocking, to say the least. Let's examine the facts. Among other dangerous elements, the now public agreement with Iran will lead to the following:

1. Twenty-four day warnings before each and every inspection of Iranian nuclear facilities is allowed, obviously a very powerful incentive to cheat their way to the nuclear bomb.

2. Immediate removal of sanctions, thereby infusing Iran's military coffers with billions of dollars, which it will no doubt use to finance its nuclear weapons program, as well as its terror surrogates in the Middle East and around the world.

3. A massive nuclear arms race in the Middle East, as Saudi Arabia and other Sunni Muslim nations will now seek to counter the threat from Shiite Muslim Iran.

So why would American Jews throw their support and money behind an Iran deal that clearly threatens Israel (not to mention the free world and even some Arab nations) with absolute destruction?

Sadly, a substantial portion of the American Jewish community has a knee-jerk devotion to the Democratic Party that is far more passionate than its concern for the survival of Israel. When push comes to shove, they will obediently side with Obama, Kerry, and Hillary against Israel. Their troubling disconnect from their Jewish roots in favor of the religion of dogmatic liberalism is one of the great tragedies of American Jewish life today.

The salvation for Israel and the free world will not come from the Democratic Party, which is already lining up behind Obama in support of a nuclear Iran. Those American Jews who still stand with Israel must now join forces with pro-Israel Christians, with Republicans, and with all other true friends of Israel in the Congressional fight against this dangerous agreement.

Ten Years Later: Bibi's Gush Katif?

"And I will restore my people Israel; they will rebuild the ruined cities and live in them. They will plant vineyards and drink their wine; they will make gardens and eat their fruit. And they will not again be rooted out from their land that I have given them," says the Lord your God.

(Amos 9:14-15)

Ten years after the tragic destruction of Gush Katif and several other Jewish communities in Gaza and northern Samaria, destroyed by the Israeli government in violation of promises to the voters, Prime Minister Benjamin (Bibi) Netanyahu and Defense Minister Moshe Ya'alon have begun implementing another brutal destruction, this time a new neighborhood in Beit El.

In the latest disregard for freedom of movement for Jews, all roads leading to Beit El were blocked by the IDF and Border Police to prevent peaceful civil disobedience by the Jewish residents of Samaria and elsewhere, who came to protest the destruction. Arabs were allowed free passage.

The irony of this obvious failure to learn from history is that the homes in question have been undergoing a legalization process that was presented to the High Court of Justice, a process that was nearing completion. Both Netanyahu and Ya'alon now say that they don't want the destruction to happen, but actions speak much louder than words. Who sent the troops? Who sent the police? Who sent the bulldozers?

The mad rush to destroy the Beit El homes is but the latest chapter in Netanyahu and Ya'alon's cynical undeclared war against Religious Zionism. Israelis remember well

Netanyahu's disingenuous pledges of support and new building permits for the Jewish residents of Judea and Samaria before last year's elections. It's also hard to forget the substantial number of votes that Netanyahu's Likud received from many thousands of supporters of Religious Zionism, who believed Netanyahu's false words.

Benjamin Netanyahu, who as Finance Minister under then Prime Minister Ariel Sharon cynically allowed the expulsion of 10,000 Jews to go forward in the summer of 2005, has betrayed this public once again, as the freeze on the granting of building permits to Jews continues. The panic that ensued before the elections, when it was feared that Yitzhak Herzog of the Zionist Union (Labor) might actually win, was unwarranted, not just because he wouldn't have been able to piece together a coalition, but also because a building freeze by Herzog wouldn't have been worse than a building freeze by Netanyahu. The current situation is that the Likud leadership has continued a defacto freeze on the granting of building permits for Jews in Judea and Samaria, while the Arabs are rapidly building Rawabi, a new city in Samaria, with full blessings and support from Netanyahu and Ya'alon.

If Netanyahu allows the destruction in Beit El, or any other destruction of Jewish communities for that matter, to go forward, the Jewish Home, which is the only party in the governing coalition that specifically supports the rebuilding of Judea and Samaria, should seriously consider leaving the coalition, Zionism is, by definition, the rebuilding of the Land of Israel by the Jewish people. An Israeli government that betrays Zionism by freezing Jewish building in the Land, while allowing Israel's enemies to grow and expand has lost its right to exist.

Legal Tyranny of the Left

"I will not acquiesce to an imperial court any more than our founders acquiesced to an imperial British monarch. We must resist and reject judicial tyranny, not retreat."

(Mike Huckabee, American politician)

I s the State of Israel being unjustly ruled by a left-wing self-perpetuating Supreme Court? This is the question that should be asked by lawmakers, after the Court ordered the destruction of residential apartment buildings in the town of Beit El in Samaria, despite the fact that legal permits had already been issued for the buildings in question.

After the destruction, which was cheered on by amused "Palestinian" Arab spectators in the neighboring city of Ramallah, an enraged MK Moti Yogev (Jewish Home) strongly criticized the Court. "Despite the valid zoning plan and the construction permit, the High Court ruled unjustly, in a way befitting charlatans. A D9 (bulldozer) shovel should be used against the High Court," he added. "We, as a legislative system, will make sure to rein in the legalistic rule in this country, and the tail that wags the dog."

As could be expected, Yogev's remarks, obviously metaphoric flair used for effect, and not intended to be taken literally, have aroused some harsh calls from the Left for his removal from the Knesset and even imprisonment. From the self-righteous agitators on the Left, who don't believe in freedom of speech for those on the Right, such arrogant yelps of anger are the norm. What is more disturbing are the arrows aimed at Yogev by government officials like Public Security Minister Gilad Erdan (Likud), who warned that disrespecting the courts could lead to the breakdown of the rule of law and "anarchy." Equally troubling is Jewish Home leader Naftali Bennett's unnecessary public comment that he "privately reprimanded" Yogev.

The main individuals who need "reprimanding", and more, are the justices of the Supreme Court, who are ruling the country as dictators, as well as Israel's political leadership that obediently adheres to such tyranny without changing the corrupt judge selection system that allows such abuse. The fact is that MK Yogev accurately expressed the frustration of a substantial amount of the Israeli population that is sick and tired of seeing its soldiers and police, paid from taxpayer funds, as tools for the destruction of Jewish communities in the heart of Israel. A Supreme Court that is not elected by the people, that even has serving justices on its own selection committee, is an anti-democratic body that does not represent the will of the people.

Such tyranny of the Supreme Court is totally unacceptable in a country that considers itself a part of the free world.

Stop Pandering to the LGBT

"The liberal idea of tolerance is more and more a kind of intolerance."

(Slavoj Zizek, Slovenian philosopher)

The stabbing attack on participants at last week's Gay Pride March in Jerusalem should be condemned, and in fact, was condemned by most public officials. Violence against peaceful marchers is criminal and is simply the wrong way to relate to those who disagree with you. Nonetheless, does that make the marchers worthy of financial support?

Most citizens of Israel would agree that the Jihadist approach of attacking those who disagree with you, as practiced in much of the Islamic world, is not the Jewish way to resolve disagreements. The sick individual who carried out the attack in Jerusalem will be incarcerated once again, and the prison system that released him, obviously without proper rehabilitation, should be investigated.

Even so, the misguided over-reactions by a few usually clear-minded politicians has been disturbing. Education Minister Naftali Bennett (Jewish Home) quickly responded to the stabbing attack by ordering a massive enlargement of funds for Israel's gay youth organization, in a surprising move given his party's firm stand against gay marriage. Yes, education towards peaceful discourse and against violence is a positive thing. No peaceful individuals should be attacked in the streets of Jerusalem. If the funds would only go towards preventing future acts of random violence towards "the other", it would be a good move.

However, most of the worldwide LGBT (Lesbian, Gay, Bisexual, and Transgender) organizations have a much broader, even aggressive political agenda that goes way beyond ensuring individual freedom. In recent years, that agenda has intimidated many Americans, restricting freedom of speech and religious expression by those who oppose same-sex marriage, and ultimately leading to the recent US Supreme Court decision legalizing gay marriage.

Israelis should be concerned, as well. In a blatant show of LGBT intolerance, and as evidence of the aggressive focus on that political agenda, Minister Bennett – along with Jewish Home MK Yinon Magal – were reportedly prevented from attending the Tel Aviv rally by the Israeli National LGBT Task Force, while Energy and Water Minister Yuval Steinitz (Likud), who did attend in support of the LGBT community was booed offstage by thousands of attendees. Only those public figures on the Left were allowed to participate, because they support "the agenda," which aims to fundamentally change society by blurring gender identities, eventually leading to public acceptance and legalization of gay marriage in Israel, giving such sexual deviations an equal social status as the traditional family structure, the marriage bond between a man and a woman.

Social laws in a society are based on values, which generally are based on the heritage of the civilization. The traditional family and traditional religious social values are under attack in Western civilization. The international LGBT movement, as an integral part of the Left, is at the forefront of those attacks, which often are quite aggressive, and in some cases, even violent.

Funding the teaching of tolerance can be very positive, but only if it is under the careful auspices of Israel's Education Ministry and if it has a narrow non-political focus, emphasizing the importance of kindness and of peaceful discourse in a civil society. Funding LGBT organizations that have a long term, malicious political agenda is a mistake that Bennett should seriously reconsider.

Adopting The Levy Report: Who Owns the Land of Israel?

"Building by Israel in Judea and Samaria does not violate the Geneva Convention. In contrast, Israel, as the representative of the Jewish people, can claim a historic right to build in Judea and Samaria. No one can deny this historic right."

(Alan Baker, Member of the Levy Committee)

In recent years, we have seen a string of Supreme Court rulings in Israel that have invariably sided with Arab claimants in land disputes in Judea and Samaria. From where do these disputes arise and who are these previously-unknown land owners who present documents supposedly proving land ownership?

After Israel's War of Independence in 1948, Judea and Samaria fell into Arab hands, specifically the Hashemite monarchy that had been placed in control by the British colonial power over what was then being called Trans-Jordan (across the Jordan). The name referred to the relatively vast land on the eastern side of the Jordan River that we read about in the Bible. Trans-Jordan, now simply called Jordan, is actually the eastern Land of Israel, where the biblical tribes Reuven, Gad, and half of Menasseh chose to establish their communities. Due to its 1948 conquest, this "country" also controlled Judea and Samaria (the western side of the Jordan River) from 1948-1967.

In the period leading up to the Six Day War of 1967, when Israel recaptured these regions, King Hussein of Jordan, seeking to curry favor with his subjects, as well as to deny future Israeli land claims, issued many deeds of land ownership to the inhabitants of his kingdom.

Jumping ahead a few decades, numerous land claims have been filed via Israel's Supreme Court by Arab claimants, descendants or even distant relatives of those individuals who had received Jordanian documents "proving" their land ownership. But are they really the owners or was King Hussein simply handing over stolen property?

Obviously, for a believing Jew, the question of land ownership is a moot point, as the biblical narrative is clear: God gave the Land of Israel to His people Israel as a divine inheritance. However, because of differing views of the biblical narrative, even within Israel, such an argument doesn't carry much weight in a court of law. In our current system of national or international law, we need to examine the full historical, political, and legal picture. The land ownership dispute rests ultimately on the legal status of land in Judea and Samaria. Whose land is it?

The 2012 Levy Report, officially known as the Report on the Legal Status of Building in Judea and Samaria is an 89 page report on the Jewish communities in Judea and Samaria. It was published on July 9, 2012 after extensive legal and historical research by a three member committee, authorized by Prime Minister Benjamin Netanyahu, commissioned by Israel's government, and headed by former Israeli Supreme Court justice Edmund Levy.

Using strictly legal arguments and based on the documented history of the region, the Levy Report proved conclusively that the Jewish presence in Judea and Samaria is legal according to international law. Nonetheless, its conclusions have yet to be adopted as policy by the Israeli government.

The various Arab land grabs are simply that – attempts to claim that which is not theirs, not historically and not legally. And that, of course, is the Hebrew meaning of the word "Palestinian" – one who invades, robs, and takes that which doesn't belong to him.

Therefore, even if we intentionally put aside what might be referred to as the "religious arguments", meaning legitimate biblical, historical claims buttressing Israel's right to establish communities in Judea and Samaria, the modern legal research clearly shows that Israel has the right to allow Jews to move to these regions and to build communities there. Recent revisionist spin notwithstanding, the international legal basis, sanction, and indeed, encouragement for Jewish settlement was there – from the Balfour Declaration, from the San Remo Peace Conference and from the League of Nations. The Levy Report simply confirmed what was already known decades earlier.

The Israel government has the power to end such recent national embarrassments as the destruction of the apartment buildings in Beit El, the imminent demolition of the twenty-year-old synagogue in Givat Ze'ev, and the evacuation of other thriving Israeli communities, all of which have been based on faulty Arab land claims. Prime Minister Benjamin Netanyahu can put an end to this historical injustice by immediately allowing the Israeli Cabinet to vote on the adoption of the Levy Report as the legal basis for government policy in Judea and Samaria.

Huckabee: Standing With Israel in Ancient Shiloh

"The entire congregation of the children of Israel assembled at Shiloh and they set up the Tent of Meeting there."

(Joshua 18:1)

Two years ago, I had the privilege of being interviewed as a guest on Mike Huckabee's radio show. It was a warm conversation with the media personality and former governor of Arkansas who had been a candidate for President of the United States in 2008, but even though some of our discussion was about politics, it wasn't the political talk that made an impression on me.

What struck me then was that I didn't feel like I was speaking to a politician, rather to a humble man who believes in God, in family, and in the biblical principles on which his country was founded. Yet it goes way beyond that, because Mike Huckabee, now once again a presidential candidate, is a passionate supporter of Israel. For Huckabee, standing with Israel isn't just a slogan. When he is asked whether a supports a Palestinian state, he says "That depends on where you want to establish such a state", clearly implying that establishing such an Islamic terrorist state in the biblical heartland of Israel – Judea and Samaria – the so-called West Bank – would be an unmitigated disaster for the survival of Israel and for the cause of freedom around the world. His common sense approach to foreign affairs tells him that such an entity would quickly become the main headquarters for local and worldwide Islamic terrorism.

The field of Republican candidates tends to be moderately

pro-Israel, with most candidates strongly opposing the Iran nuclear deal that the Obama administration has been trying to ram down Congressional throats before they read its sordid details. However, only one of the candidates is on the record as opposing the poisonous "land for peace" formula that calls on Israel to surrender its historic, biblical heartland to the Fatah and Hamas terrorists of the Palestinian Authority.

It's relatively easy in the court of American public opinion to say that Israel "has a right to exist", but it takes much more courage and integrity to stand against the attempts to carve up Israel into pieces. Governor Huckabee has the courage of his convictions and he proved it once again today by visiting Ancient Shiloh in the heart of Samaria. Shiloh was the capital of Israel for 369 years in the days of Joshua, Hannah, and Samuel the Prophet. In fact, the great biblical leader, Joshua, spoke to the current "Palestinian State challenge" 3,300 years before its time, proclaiming to the Israelites (Joshua 18:3), "How long will you wait, before coming to take possession of the Land that the Lord, God of your fathers has given you?"

That challenge remains before us today, as the world pressure on Jewish rights in the biblical heartland of Israel is increasing every day. Will the free world stand with Israel against the forces of darkness? Hopefully, we will soon see how the other presidential candidates will stake their ground on this issue, but at least one candidate has made his position clear, and therefore, I wish Governor Mike Huckabee great success in 2016!

US Dems Fail the Litmus Test

"Never before has a US president and a political party consented to funding the enemy."

(Mark Levin, American talk radio host)

Since the signing of the nuclear deal with Iran, I have been warning that even if Congress had rejected this dangerous agreement, the damage would have already been done, as the Russians, the Chinese, and the Europeans are already preparing big business with ayatollahs.

However, the vote on the deal has become a litmus test for the new Democratic Party, as the anti-Israel, anti-America ideologues of the far left have taken over what was once the party of President Harry Truman, a great lover of Israel, to the extent that most Democratic senators are afraid to actively oppose President Obama's strong support for the Iran deal.

As of today, there is no longer any doubt. The deal will go through without the need for a presidential veto. Democratic Senators Richard Blumenthal (CT), Gary Peters (MI), and Ron Wyden (OR) have all just announced support for the deal, after which they immediately went through the now all-too-familiar ritual of trying to publicly justify their yes votes.

> "While this is not the agreement I would have accepted at the negotiating table, it is better than no deal at all," Blumenthal insisted.

> "This agreement with the duplicitous and untrustworthy Iranian regime falls short of what I had envisioned, however I have decided the

alternatives are even more dangerous," Wyden wrote.

Oh, really? An agreement with a "duplicitous and untrustworthy" regime that allows them over 24 days warning before an inspection of nuclear facilities is less dangerous than what?

Let's call a spade a spade. The Democrats have thrown Israel to the wolves to save their own political skin because the Dems are no longer pro-Israel. They are supporting a president who has pushed forward a foolish nuclear agreement that not one major political player in Israel – left, right, or center – is supporting. What does that tell you?

For one thing, it tells me that the Democrats are pro-Israel in name only. Why were there no Democrats demanding that Obama give Israel passive military support to help it launch a preemptive strike on Iran's nuclear research facilities? Most Israelis understand that a nuclear Iran will be an existential threat to Israel, and therefore, those American Democrats who have stood firmly with their anti-Israel president against America's staunchest ally and against America's long-term security, should be exposed for the political whores that they are. And that includes a few Jewish senators whose only religious belief seems to be a dogmatic left-wing ideology that is a sick remnant of the 1960s' anti-war movement. There is nothing less Jewish than a knee-jerk belief that any deal is better than military action and that there is never a good military option.

Israel should launch a massive lightning preemptive strike on Iran and the US should passively support its ally with any weapons that are needed to effectively do the job. Clearly, that's not going to happen with this president or any Democrat, so the question remains whether Israel will go it alone, perhaps with quiet logistical support from Saudi Arabia, which is so terrified of a nuclear Iran that it may be willing to ignore its reflexive Muslim hatred of Israel.

Barring that intriguing possibility, will we have to wait for a Republican president to stand with Israel? Will America's suicidal Jews continue to vote for the Democrat?

Syrian Refugees – Western Guilt

"We've seen those results in generations of Muslim immigrants – farmers and factory workers, helping to lay the railroads and build our cities, the Muslim innovators who helped build some of our highest skyscrapers and who helped unlock the secrets of our universe."

(Barack Hussein Obama, American President)

The pressure is on for the free world to welcome in the Syrian refugees, who are fleeing that country's civil war in droves, probably joined by thousands of fellow Muslims from other countries, looking for safe passage to the West. As the Muslim world implodes, an international guilt trip is being hoisted upon the leaders of the US, and especially on the European countries. British Prime Minister David Cameron's pledge this week to take in 20,000 refugees from Syria by 2020 has been slammed by critics as inadequate. Surprisingly, there were even defensive, apologetic responses this week from Republican anti-illegal immigration presidential candidates such as Donald Trump, suggesting that he might be willing to reluctantly take in some of the refugees.

While Europe has borne the brunt of the big push, even little Israel is beginning to let its Jewish guilt get in the way of rational thinking. First in line is opposition leader Yitzhak Herzog.

"I call on the government of Israel to act toward receiving refugees from the war in Syria, in addition to the humanitarian efforts it is already making," Herzog said. "Jews cannot be indifferent while hundreds of thousands of refugees are looking for safe haven."

Seizing on that theme, Jewish universal immigration organizations such as HIAS, which once focused on Jewish immigration needs, are now advocating for a mass welcome for the latest illegal Muslim immigrants, urging the US government to take in some 100,000.

Herzog and HIAS notwithstanding, some left-leaning public figures aren't joining the "Let Them In" movement. Israeli opposition politician Yair Lapid stated yesterday that "Israel, unfortunately, cannot allow itself into the refugee crisis issue. It's a European issue and there's no reason we should be part of it."

Nonetheless, even that statement misses the point and misidentifies the guilty party. It's not a European issue, nor is it an American issue, and it's certainly not an Israeli or Jewish issue. It is wholly about a destructive bedlam in an Islamic world that has run amok and is imploding before our very eyes. Even so, the wealthy Islamic nations in the Persian Gulf, vast in territory and vaster in resources, are closing their eyes, and their borders. Why should the free world take in additional Muslim refugees with all of the serious demographic and security challenges that they cause, while Saudi Arabia, the self-acclaimed leader of Islam, refuses to open its borders and its pocketbook?

The long-term survival of the West and of course, of Israel, requires the immediate closure of borders to further deter Islamic immigration and the expulsion of those who have entered illegally. This is an internal Muslim issue, a crisis that they have created on their own, and it should be treated as such.

The Newest Islamic Tsunami

"Those (refugees) who enter Europe are almost all Muslims, and behave as some Muslims often do in the Muslim world: they harass Christians and attack women … more than 75% of those who arrive are men under 50; few are women, children or elders. Rapes, assaults, stabbings and other crimes are on the rise."

(Report from the Gatestone Institute)

As the Muslim refugees continue to flood into Europe and, to a lesser extent, North America, there are increasing reports from multiple disparate sources that a large minority, and perhaps even a majority, of the immigrants seeking asylum are not really Syrian refugees, but are actually economic/political immigrants seeking to exploit the chaos in Syria for their own purposes.

The inexplicable European eagerness, especially in countries like Germany and Sweden, which already suffer from large and rapidly growing Muslim minorities, to absorb hundreds of thousands of new Muslim immigrants into their populations, is quite bizarre in its suicidal blindness.

Despite evidence to the contrary, this Islamic tsunami is still being falsely billed as a chance for the West to help the suffering Syrian refugees. However, Iraqis, Libyans, Pakistanis, Egyptians, and even so-called Palestinians are attempting to pass themselves off as Syrian, in order to arouse the misguided guilt of the free world. This is now being reported increasingly by aid workers, government officials and fellow immigrants.

The doors of Saudi Arabia are closed. The doors of Qatar are closed. The doors of Dubai are closed. Therefore, it's hard to believe, indeed, that the old continent of Europe, which has gradually been evolving into Eurabia in recent years with the dual cancers of Muslim street violence and anti-Semitism spreading like wildfire, will continue its self-destruction, by welcoming in droves those who will ultimately make the oppressive, misogynistic, and intolerant Islamic Sharia the law of their lands.

Therefore, it is imperative that North America, in addition to any European countries that may have resisted up to this point, quickly close its doors to the new Islamic tsunami. This is not a humanitarian issue. It's a demographic invasion.

Lastly, I would strongly suggest to those still-free nations that want to survive as such: Stop pandering to an Islamic world that seeks to destroy Western civilization. Stand with freedom. End your foolish boycotts of Israel and your near-sighted deals with the enemies of Israel. Putting aside the sad history of anti-Semitic persecution in many of your countries, remember that Israel is the one nation in the Middle East that will fight bravely against the sword of Jihad, which is attempting to bring down both of our houses.

Threats from the Arab Moderates

"I promise to crush Israel and return it to the humiliation and wretchedness of the Koran."

(Anwar Sadat, President of Egypt who initiated the 1973 Yom Kippur war, and several years later was assassinated by his own countrymen after signing a peace agreement with Israel.)

What is an Arab (Muslim) moderate? Is such a term an oxymoron, or does the media consist of morons who routinely use such a term to refer to the leaders of countries/entities such as Egypt, Jordan, and the Palestinian Authority?

Within forty-eight hours, two supposed Arab moderate leaders are threatening Israel. Jordan's King Abdullah is warning of an "explosion" on the Temple Mount, accusing Israel of "provocations" and is threatening to "take action" should Israel not refrain from protecting non-Muslim visitors to the site where the Holy Temple of Israel stood for hundreds of years.

> "It is without doubt a dangerous violation of Islamic holy places," Egyptian President Abdel Fattah al-Sisi said of Israeli subsequent law enforcement at a press conference with EU President Donald Tusk, urging Israel to take "immediate and effective steps" to defuse tensions.

What remains unstated by these so-called moderates is that the Islamic structures on the Temple Mount were intentionally built on the ruins of the Holy Temple, both to hide the ruins from the Jewish site and to show the triumph of Islam over the Jews. Not a very noble or moral intention, especially given that the Jews were sovereign in Jerusalem many hundreds of years before the rise of Islam some fourteen hundred years ago.

Furthermore, the Arab leaders' transparently self-serving statements have been uttered in the wake of many months of organized violent attacks and brutal harassment by Muslim worshippers on Jewish and other visitors to the holy site. The Israeli police have finally been ordered not just to protect the Jewish visitors from outright injury, but to actually stop the harassment.

Therefore, the pugnacious comments by Sisi and Abdullah have no basis in reality, unless one includes the sick reality of Islamic knee-jerk bias against Israel. True Sisi and Abdullah don't like Hamas, but their natural Islamic hatred of Israel is apparently much stronger than their moderate images might lead one to believe. A true moderate wouldn't criticize freedom of worship for Jews on their holiest site, nor would he make veiled threats of violence against Israelis for defending those basic rights.

In fact, the verbal warfare began just a couple of days prior, when Palestinian Authority (PA) Chairman Mahmoud Abbas, called for violence at the Temple Mount against Jews saying: "The Al-Aqsa (Temple Mount) is ours ... and they (Jews) have no right to defile it with their filthy feet." These words were spoken by the man that the Israeli elites fondly call "Abu Mazen", the Israeli Left's beloved, and, oh so moderate partner for peace.

Moderates, indeed...

Ben Carson and Muslims in the White House

"I shall terrorize the infidels. So wound their bodies and incapacitate them because they oppose Allah and his Apostle (Muhammad)."

(Koran 8:12)

American presidential candidate, Dr. Ben Carson, has been viciously attacked recently for his affirmative answer to an interviewer, in which he was asked if he would find it difficult to support a Muslim candidate for president. This provocative question was asked of Carson just a day after fellow candidate Donald Trump had failed to criticize a questioning audience member at a town hall gathering, who specifically stated that President Obama is a Muslim.

Focusing just on the Carson statement, was it really a racist or bigoted remark, as some of his critics allege? Can a person's religious beliefs impinge a candidate's worthiness? Later clarifying his statement, Carson emphasized that Islamic Sharia law is contrary to the American Constitution. Nonetheless, the cabal of Islamic ideologues and their usual leftist allies have been unceasing in their verbal lynch of the good doctor, who hasn't got a racist bone in his body.

Fact: Sharia law is central in Islam.

Fact: Jihad, or holy war against non-Muslims, is central in Islam.

Let's examine just a few inconvenient facts about Sharia law:

1. Sharia permits wife-beating.

2. Sharia doesn't allow the building or renovation of any place of worship other than a mosque.

3. Sharia calls for cutting off the hands of shoplifters.

4. Sharia calls for the murder of a Muslim who changes his religion.

5. Sharia calls for the murder of those who publicly criticize Muhammad (the founder of Islam) and the Koran (the "Bible" of Islam).

Those are just a few highlights of the system of law that is dominant in leading Muslim countries, like Saudi Arabia and Iran. Is that really the kind of law that the free world wants to import?

Ben Carson lives in a country that believes in free speech. There is no question that he should be permitted to voice his apprehension on this issue. The political rise of American Muslims, who in most cases don't believe in the basic Judeo-Christian tenets on which the United States was founded, would indeed be a serious danger to the freedoms that Americans often take for granted. Carson was correct in pointing that out.

The Diplomatic Solution – Again

"The definition of insanity is doing the same thing over and over again and expecting different results."

(Albert Einstein, physicist)

After a multiple rocket attack was fired in the direction of the city of Ashdod, and fortunately was stopped by the Iron Dome defensive system, MK Haim Yellin (Yesh Atid) is calling on Prime Minister Binyamin Netanyahu to take action against the renewed rocket fire from Gaza. As with most such demands from the Left, he isn't demanding a strong military response. In fact, Yellin is actually calling for "a diplomatic solution" – Israeli code words for another "peace process."

With whom is he suggesting that we make peace and on what terms? Of course, he doesn't specify, since to do so would make him the laughing stock of the Knesset. Let's examine the two options for peace partners:

- Hamas – The Islamic terrorist organization is willing to hold back the rocket fire only if Israel pays ransom, often called financial assistance, which will be used to purchase weapons, to build new weapons/terrorist smuggling tunnels, and to fund other "urgent needs."

- Fatah – Previously led by the father of modern terrorism, Yasser Arafat, Fatah is now headed by noted Holocaust denier Mahmoud Abbas, who has continued and expanded the not-so-diplomatic tradition of placing all terrorists on the payroll of his Palestinian Authority, provided that they accomplish the great deed of killing or wounding Jews.

In short, those Israelis who demand "diplomatic solutions" are either dishonest or ignorant. The only peace process that can work is one that is based on full Israeli sovereignty over the lands currently in its possession, with full civil rights granted only to peaceful residents, with the possibility of citizenship for those who prove themselves worthy. Those who continue to agitate against the Jewish state have no right to be here and must be deported.

Given that the two prospective partners cited above are not ready to even consider such a peace-enhancing scenario, to speak repeatedly about pie-in-the-sky "diplomatic solutions" is a fool's paradise at best. It's hard to believe that there are Knesset members that still wear rose-colored glasses in light of the Islamic aggression that is trying to kill us all.

Abbas: Murderer – Again

"It's time that we stop babbling about talking directly to Abbas, as if he is simply an estranged spouse."

(David Rubin, author of this book)

As Israel bitterly mourns another two parent victims of Islamic terror and as their bewildered four young children are forced to bury their parents, Senior Fatah official Mahmoud Al-Aloul, a member of the Fatah Central Committee, has proudly declared that the Fatah terrorist group, led by Palestinian Authority Chairman Mahmoud Abbas, is responsible for the heinous murder of Rabbi Eitam and Naama Henkin yesterday in Samaria.

Over and over, Prime Minister Benjamin Netanyahu proclaims his desire to "sit and talk directly" with Abbas, who he insists on calling by his humanizing nickname, "Abu Mazen", but there is nothing human about this savage beast, who sometimes calls for peace and always delivers death.

When will our political leaders stop trying to be politically correct in the eyes of a world that seeks our destruction? The actual killer wasn't acting alone. He was sent by Abbas, the master terrorist with the mustache and the tie, who is warmly welcomed in every world capital.

A savage is a savage and an enemy is an enemy. Nothing has changed, nor will it change until we start acting like a proud people that believes in its right to this land.

It's time that we stop babbling about talking directly to Abbas, as if he is simply an estranged spouse. Instead, let's start attacking his Palestinian-occupied cities to such a forceful extent that he will soon plead for mercy. Then we can finally dictate the terms of his surrender and the dissolution of his corrupt, evil Palestinian Authority.

Sending him to a friendly country like Syria would be a good next step.

Want to Crush the Terrorism?
Crush the Mukata!

"If you are not prepared to use force to defend civilization, be prepared to accept barbarism."

(Thomas Sowell, American economist)

In response to the sharp upsurge in terrorism against Israeli civilians, particularly in Samaria and in Jerusalem, the Israeli Cabinet has announced a series of security measures designed to stop the terrorist attacks that have left eleven children orphaned in just three days. These measures include legal steps that will enable the Israeli government to speedily destroy the homes of the terrorists who perform such horrific attacks.

An objective observer should be forgiven for wondering why the primary target of these security measures should just be the terrorists who pulled the trigger or threw the rock. After all, weren't they sent by somebody? Aren't they being paid and encouraged to carry out these attacks?

The Palestinian Authority, led by Mahmoud Abbas, has been the true culprit behind these attacks. Millions of shekels have been flowing to each terrorist by Abbas and his henchman, continuing and expanding an infamous tradition begun by Abbas's predecessor, Yasser Arafat. Furthermore, many streets have been named after assorted Hamas, Fatah, and Islamic Jihad terrorists and baby-killers.

So who is really responsible and what should be done about it? I, for one, am sick and tired of reading the statements of Israeli politicians proclaiming the tentative, defensive security steps that they will now take to stop the terrorists from committing their dastardly deeds. Will they continue those steps indefinitely, or will they soon announce an easing of the steps after a couple of weeks of quiet, so as to "maintain a normal lifestyle for Palestinian civilians", after which two more Israeli parents may be gunned down as their young children watch in terror?

By not cutting off the head of the snake, we are encouraging future acts of terror. The head of the snake is the terrorist headquarters of the Palestinian Authority, the Mukata in Ramallah, and that should be the next target for Israeli retaliation and deterrence. That is where the planning and funding of the terrorism happens. Until we conquer and destroy the Mukata, seizing its leaders, weapons, and documents, no Israeli crackdown will be taken seriously.

Why wait until the next Israeli parent or child is killed?

Bibi: No New Building Permits for Jews

"See, the Lord your God has given you the land. Go up and take possession of it as the Lord, God of your fathers, told you. Do not be afraid; do not be discouraged."

(Deuteronomy 1:21)

In my previous article, I emphasized that terrorist orders come from the top – from Hamas, from Fatah, and from their Palestinian Authority (PA). Aside from the immediate purpose of killing and wounding Jews, the goal of the PA leadership is clear – to instill fear among the Jewish population so that Jews will be afraid to live in or even visit Judea, Samaria, and Jerusalem.

Our response to the terrorists, aside from a strong offensive military response, should be that not only will we not run away, but that we will continue to rebuild the biblical heartland of Israel. Now is the time to be building new Jewish cities and towns in the mountains of Judea and Samaria, as well as strengthening the existing ones. However, the message from Prime Minister Benjamin (Bibi) Netanyahu has been exactly the opposite. In a closed-door meeting with political leaders from Judea and Samaria, Netanyahu made it clear that he will not authorize any new building in response to the terrorism. Claiming the difficulty of dealing with European pressure and threats of United Nations resolutions, Bibi refused to allow new permits for Jewish building, despite the fact that he has authorized and forcefully pushed forward the construction of Rawabi, a new Arab city in Samaria.

This is the same Netanyahu that cynically ran after nationalistic voters of the Jewish Home party before the elections pleading for their votes. Yes, the same slick Netanyahu that praised the Jewish communities of the biblical heartland, before the elections, but now refuses to authorize the building of one Jewish home.

MK's of the Jewish Home party should not fear Netanyahu's empty threats to fire them for criticizing his obvious failure to fight terrorism and his absolute failure to build. Such pusillanimous behavior in refusing to build should be criticized forcefully by the elected representatives of the nationalist public. If Bibi's current threats to fire them cause them to be silent, they will rightly be accused of clinging to their cushy ministerial posts, as the Jewish residents of Judea, Samaria, and Jerusalem are harshly choked for lack of places to live.

Bibi's discrimination against the Jews of the biblical heartland is shameful, and his weakness towards Israel's enemies is pathetic. The policy of freezing new building for Jews is totally his (with the help of his sidekick Defense Minister Moshe Ya'alon), but those in the Cabinet who silently acquiesce will share some of the blame. What is most disturbing is that the terrorists will hear the message loud and clear.

A Recipe for Israel's Survival

"Victory at all costs, victory in spite of all terror, victory however long and hard the road may be; for without victory, there is no survival."

(Winston Churchill, British statesman)

On a day in which the Arabs launched terror attacks in Jerusalem, Petach Tikvah, Jaffa, Samaria, Judea, Kiryat Gat, and Maale Adumim, Israel's political leadership is still acting as if the Palestinian Authority is our "Partner for Peace."

The Israeli and PA military liaison committees met this morning to "discuss ways of preventing an escalation." Coordinator of Government Activities in Judea and Samaria, Major-General Yoav Mordechai, today announced to Palestinian Authority (PA) media that Israel is not interested in an escalation of the security situation in Judea and Samaria, and that Israel is maintaining the status quo on the Temple Mount. Mordechai went on to assure the PA media that the police had eased restrictions on PA Arab entry to the Temple Mount during the fall holiday season.

No escalation? Are we really interested in maintaining the current status quo of Jews being attacked in the heart of Jerusalem and throughout the Land of Israel?

Has Israel's leadership forgotten who sent it to the Knesset and whose rights it needs to be protecting? The PA media and the PA military have incited the latest wave of terrorism. They are Israel's enemy, no less than Iran, and they should be treated as such.

Let us be clear: No security measures will be effective in the long run, until Israel's political leadership makes a political decision to destroy the Palestinian Authority. But how does one go about doing that?

1. Announce to the world that from this day onward, the Oslo Accords and the PA which it created are null and void.

2. Send the IDF into every PA controlled city in Judea and Samaria.

3. Seize control and take away all of their weapons.

4. Destroy the Mukata, the PA headquarters in Ramallah, and seize all computers and documents, which will prove their complicity in the recent terrorism.

5. Assert full Israeli control over Judea and Samaria.

6. Declare the Levy Report, which in 2012 proved the legal basis for Jewish sovereignty in Judea and Samaria, to be the basis for government policy in "the territories."

7. Pass a law demanding the expulsion of anyone found guilty of launching a terror attack against Israeli citizens.

8. Declare and enable the immediate resumption of the granting of new building projects for Jews in Judea, Samaria, and Jerusalem.

9. Freeze all building in any town or village from which the terror attacks have emanated.

10. Extend all of the above to the Gaza region.

Clearly, this would need to be done swiftly, with no hesitation. It would also need to be accompanied by a massive public relations campaign, but we need not fear empty threats and UN resolutions. If we exude confidence and do not apologize for protecting Israel's right to live securely in its God-given land, many will accept our message. Those who won't, don't accept our message even now, as we pander to the haters and struggle to convince the world how well we look after Arab rights.

Compromise and apologies won't bring security. For once, let's be strong, courageous, and defend the complete Land of Israel!

Revenge Attacks on Arabs: Should We Be Concerned?

"If you prick us do we not bleed? If you tickle us do we not laugh? If you poison us do we not die? And if you wrong us shall we not revenge?"

(William Shakespeare, British poet, playwright, and actor)

After over a week of many Islamic terror attacks, which have included many horrific murders and wounding of Jewish men, women, and children, including shootings, rock attacks, and stabbings, we now are hearing reports of a couple of attacks or attempted attacks by Jews against Arabs, one of the suspects being a young woman who is accused of spraying an Arab with mace. Neither of the cases compares to the scores of vicious attacks carried out against Jews that have been an almost hourly occurrence throughout the Land of Israel, but it does raise the question of why the reverse might even happen. Why would Jews feel the need to take the law into their own hands?

For about twenty years, the Palestinian Authority (PA) has led the mostly-Muslim Arabs of the Land of Israel in a terrorist war of Jihad (holy war) against the Jews. The PA was created as a result of the Oslo Accords, which were signed by Israel and the Palestine Liberation Organization's Yasser Arafat, the father of modern terrorism. Their current leader, Mahmoud Abbas, has continued and expanded its policy of inciting, encouraging, and financing terrorist attacks against Israelis.

With 78% of Israelis expressing their disapproval of Netanyahu's handling of the security situation, it's quite evident that many Israelis are angry, and rightly so. The latest terror wave has an address, the Mukata in Ramallah, the headquarters of the PA. Despite this fact, Prime Minister Benjamin (Bibi) Netanyahu and Defense Minister Moshe (Bogie) Ya'alon share a strange propensity for blaming "the settlers", implying that the right-wing Jewish residents of Judea, Samaria, and Jerusalem, who have suffered disproportionately from the terrorism, and others on the right who share their views, are somehow at fault for the dastardly deeds of Abbas and his henchmen.

According to the bizarre rhetoric of Netanyahu and Ya'alon:

- How dare those uppity settlers and their right-wing fellow countrymen demand that Israel's government actually hold the PA accountable for its actions and take offensive action against it!

- How dare those uppity settlers and their right-wing fellow countrymen demand that Israel's government allow the building of Jewish homes in the historical biblical heartland of Israel!

While all right-wing Israelis are apparently typecast as "settlers" (as if there is something wrong with being a pioneer in rebuilding your national home) by Bibi and Bogie and Israel's "lamestream" media, it should be noted that the couple of attacks against Arabs have not been carried out in Judea, nor have they been carried out in Samaria. These few attacks, which may indeed be proven to be acts of self-defense, even if not supported by most Israelis, are a clear sign that the people are very frustrated by their government's ineptitude, and the recent polls are proof of that.

Could it possibly be that Israelis throughout the country are getting fed up with the Likud, being led by a Bibi-

Bogie team that is so inexplicably terrified of toothless UN resolutions that they are afraid to take firm action against Israel's enemies?

Could it be that Israel's leaders are so fearful of UN resolutions that they will continue their suicidal rush to build new Arab cities, like Rawabi in Samaria, while conversely continuing a freeze on new building in historical Jewish cities like Jerusalem, Shiloh, and Hebron?

Individual random attacks on Arabs will certainly not stop the terrorism. Bold leadership by Israel's government will. We will win this war against the Islamic terrorists when our government stops fearing UN resolutions, EU declarations, and US diktats. A nation that proudly rebuilds its land and boldly crushes its enemies will win the respect of the world, if not its love (that will come much later). Most importantly, if Netanyahu finally agrees to take strong offensive action while ignoring international condemnation, the people of Israel, along with its many friends in North America and some other parts of the world, will stand with him.

No More Fear: Time To Respond!

"And the Lord said to Joshua, Do not fear them, for I have given them into your hands. Not a man of them shall stand before you."

(Joshua 10:8)

I was actually a bit amused yesterday to read that Fatah's arch-terrorist Marwan Barghouti quoted the great Jewish scientist Albert Einstein's famous quote that the definition of insanity is doing the same thing over and over again and expecting different results. The media-friendly Barghouti, currently serving several terms of life imprisonment for masterminding mass murders of Jews in the streets of Israel, actually was quoting the right Jew in this case, and there is much that we can learn from that quote in confronting the latest terror wave that is raging in the streets of Israel.

That terror wave, by the way, is being masterminded, and most likely financed by the Fatah terrorist organization, led by Mahmoud Abbas and Barghouti, as the heir apparent, if not for the inconvenient fact that he's in jail. As reported by Palestinian Media Watch, Fatah leaders have been publicly praising the terrorists who have carried out the most recent shootings and stabbings as "martyrs" and "heroes." Among others, Fatah Central Committee member Mahmoud Al-Aloul called for Palestinian Arab youth to "rise up against the enemies," calling the youth "potential martyrs for the beloved Palestine."

Unlike the "cultured" Europeans, who haven't got a clue when it comes to responding to Islamic aggression, even in their own backyard, most Israelis instinctively know that the Arabs, especially the Jihadists among them, only respect those who speak their language of strength, or at least act with disproportionate force. The time for dilly-dallying, otherwise known as measured responses, has long passed. It's time to burn the ground under their feet until they raise up the white flags of surrender and plead on their knees for Jewish mercy, as they did in 1948 and 1967.

Start by flattening the Palestinian Authority's Mukata headquarters in Ramallah and the Hamas headquarters in Gaza. That's where the orders are coming from for the terror attacks. The Arabs like to promote their "days of rage," but it's all a bluff. In truth, there is no such thing as "spontaneous rage." The orders come from the terror heads and their sinister network.

It's time for the enemy to understand that Jews can also have "rage," and that Jews will be allowed to build homes throughout our land. No more fear and no more hesitation. The best defense is a good offense. Let's get started.

Would Bibi Have Met With Hitler in 1938?

"Balk the enemy's power; force him to reveal himself."

(Sun Tzu, Chinese philosopher)

In 1938, with the Holocaust on the horizon, British Prime Minister Neville Chamberlain met with Nazi Chieftain Adolf Hitler. The results of the well-intentioned Chamberlain's pusillanimous behavior towards the German bully are known to all, as WWII became unavoidable and six million Jews were slaughtered by the Nazi death machine.

Israel has suffered through hourly violence and intimidation in the latest wave of vicious terror attacks spearheaded/encouraged by Mahmoud Abbas's Palestinian Authority, led by its Fatah terrorist component, in not so subtle cooperation with Hamas and Islamic Jihad. Abbas doesn't have the bombastic charisma of a Hitler, and while his flamboyant predecessor Yasser Arafat could rightly be called the father of modern terrorism, Abbas shuns his mentor's military uniform and unconcealed weapon. Through his carefully crafted image of moderation, Abbas has managed to hoodwink most of the world with his often calm demeanor and talk of peace, while simultaneously leading a vicious terror war against Israel and using anti-Semitic imagery that would have made Hitler proud.

After more than two weeks of insisting that his coalition members remain silent and trust him to lead the nation through this crisis, the Prime Minister of Israel, Benjamin (Bibi) Netanyahu, finally addressed the nation and the world about the violence afflicting his country. What did he have to say?

First of all, he was quite critical of Abbas, whom he still strangely refers to affectionately by his nickname, Abu Mazen. He blasted him for his recent lies about the imagined death of a teenaged terrorist, who after carrying out a vicious stabbing attack, is rapidly recovering from his mild injury under the care of the best doctors in Israel. Meanwhile, his thirteen year old Jewish victim remains in serious condition, fighting for his life.

Netanyahu went on to condemn Abbas's continuing campaign of incitement, which has resulted in the death and wounding of so many Israelis in recent days. This has been obvious to all, and few Jewish Israelis would defend Abbas from such legitimate criticism. Interestingly, Netanyahu didn't say a thing about Abbas's long-time role, nor that of his Palestinian Authority, as the leading financier of the terrorists and their families, nor did he mention any significant response by Israel other than strengthened defensive measures. However, Bibi did accuse Abbas of denying the Holocaust and insisting on a "Judenrein" Palestine while "shamelessly" accusing Israel of genocide and ethnic cleansing.

Yet in the same breath, some words uttered by the PM were in the spirit of the embarrassingly obsequious Neville Chamberlain. Speaking to the world media, Netanyahu declared, "I'm willing to meet with Abbas to restore calm". Is he serious? After two weeks of hell for the average Israeli citizen, in which Jews are afraid to walk the streets of Israel's cities, Bibi is willing to meet with this Muslim Nazi so that the Obama/Kerry team in Washington won't vote to condemn Israel in UN resolutions? Does he really think that meeting Abbas will help Israel's deterrence?

As with the infamous Chamberlain-Hitler meeting, a Netanyahu-Abbas rendezvous would be perceived as weakness in the face of terror. Is that the enduring legacy that Bibi wants?

Will He Announce This In The Next Campaign?

"We have no intention of building new (Jewish) settlements or of expropriating additional land for existing settlements."

(Benjamin Netanyahu, Prime Minister of Israel)

During the last Israeli elections, Prime Minister Benjamin Netanyahu boasted loudly to potential right-wing voters that his previous term's building freeze was a thing of the past, that he would now stand strongly with the Jewish residents of Judea and Samaria if they would just help his Likud party to win. Voters heeded his appeal by the thousands, enabling a strong Likud victory. Since then, however, there has been a defacto freeze on the granting of new building permits in Judea, Samaria, and Jerusalem.

This thumb in the eyes of the Jewish residents of Judea, Samaria, and Jerusalem has been a persistent theme of the current Netanyahu government, despite his pre-election promises to the voters.

Finally, the rhetorical cat is out of the bag – Several days ago, Netanyahu proudly announced to the delegates at the World Zionist Congress in Jerusalem that his administrations have built less homes in the areas recaptured in the Six-Day War than his three predecessors – Ehud Olmert, Ariel Sharon, and Ehud Barak:

> "During my first term as prime minister, we built, on average, 3,000 housing units per year in Judea and Samaria," Netanyahu said. "When Barak was prime minister, he built 5,000 units, Sharon built

1,900 units, and Olmert built 1,700 units. In light of the circumstances, the average number of housing units built during my terms in office dropped to 1,500 per year," the premier added.

"We can have a discussion about this another time, but facts are facts. These numbers are precise. So instead of seeing a rise in settlement construction, there has actually been a drop," Netanyahu said.

After dropping that bombshell, he says, "We can have this discussion another time." I disagree.

Let's have this discussion now. Let's discuss how Netanyahu intentionally misled thousands of idealistic, but gullible voters in order to remain on his throne, and let's also have this discussion in the days leading up to the next election, when we can surely expect to see Mr. Netanyahu once again visiting pre-military academies in Samaria and happily planting trees in the hilltop communities, which he now derisively calls settlements.

Despite his tough, proud Zionist image, when it comes to building in Judea, Samaria, and Jerusalem, Netanyahu has been worse than every one of his predecessors. As he says in his own words, "Facts are facts. The numbers are precise."

Who's Afraid of the Big, Bad Putin?

"Between major countries, there certainly always are some common ground and points of tension."

(Vladimir Putin, Russian President)

Americans are very concerned about Russian President Vladimir Putin's newly announced involvement in Syria, which may be one of the main motivations for US President Barack Obama's announcement today that he is sending an initial fifty troops to Syria "to advise Syrian rebels in their struggle against ISIS." Should Israel be concerned about Putin, as well?

Perhaps the American concern is due to the stigma of what was once the Cold War between the United States and the Soviet Union. Russia, as the largest component of that now extinct Communist union, is still seen by most Americans, as a fierce competitor of the United States, and that perception has only increased as the Obama administration has retreated from its role as the undisputed leader of the free world.

Putin is an unashamedly strong leader who has been increasingly asserting Russia's strength on the world stage, and therefore, Russia's re-entry into the Middle East via Syria should come as no surprise. Syrian President Bashar Assad's fifteen years of absolute rule has been under relentless attack since 2011 in what has evolved into a chaotic multi-front civil war, during which almost 300,000 people have been killed. Whatever one thinks of the dictatorial brutality of Assad, Putin sees him as an ally, and in his eyes, an ally should be supported, which partially explains his involvement in strongly buttressing the Assad regime.

Of course, there are other motivations. Putin, like most Western leaders has a Muslim problem, as the Islamic tsunami that is engulfing Europe is slowly making its way to his shores, including not so insignificant Muslim groups that already live within the Russian Federation, such as the Chechins and Tatars. Defeating Assad's ISIS opponents would certainly be desirable from Putin's perspective, as it could stem any infiltration of ISIS extremists among his already problematic Muslim minorities. Last but certainly not least, Putin is seizing the opportunity of American weakness to make a symbolic show of strength and influence in the Middle East

These are all understandable reasons for Putin's involvement in Syria, but should Israel be concerned? Not really. Netanyahu met with Putin a couple of weeks ago in a clear expression of coordination, if not cooperation. It's extremely unlikely that Putin would cross Israel's red lines concerning Russian support for Assad, which shouldn't be extended to encompass support for the Hezbollah terrorists who have assisted their ally Assad. As can be seen from yesterday's Israeli strike on Hezbollah targets in Syria, Israel will continue to attack when needed.

As for Assad, do we really care if he regains power, but in a greatly weakened position? He is certainly not a friend of Israel, but he is probably better than the wealthy and quite extreme ISIS group. The nearly half-decade civil war in Syria has also revealed an additional hodgepodge of Sunni Muslim rebel groups, who are enemies of Assad, but also are enemies of Israel. This is the unfortunate reality here in the bad neighborhood that we call the Middle East. Aside from the Kurds, who are fighting for autonomy in the northeastern region of Syria some distance from Israel, there is no potential ally for Israel.

In short, if my enemy is fighting my enemy, let the party

continue and we need not shed any tears.

Meanwhile, we should quietly assist the Kurds from a distance and continue to keep a very close watch on the other side of our border, taking firm action when needed.

The GOP and Israel

"If you will not stand with Israel and the Jews, then I will not stand with you."

(Ted Cruz, US Senator, Republican presidential candidate)

Growing up in "progressive" New York City, I always believed that the Democrats were the only party in town. Republicans (otherwise known as the GOP, or Grand Old Party) were stereotyped as those "rednecks and hicks who live in the sticks" and no Jew in his right mind could ever dream of voting for them.

My views have evolved since then, not only on the liberal knee-jerk social issues such as abortion, same-sex marriage, and school prayer, but especially on what is rapidly becoming a major issue in the GOP – Israel.

While most politicians in Congress would claim to be pro-Israel, the overwhelming majority of Congressional Democrats voted for the Iran nuclear deal, which will enable the staunchly anti-Israel Islamic nation to acquire the nuclear bomb within ten years. That agreement was bitterly opposed by most Israelis across the political spectrum.

Furthermore, the leading Democratic candidates for president are on record as supporting an independent Palestinian state. They also oppose Israel's right to build homes in its ancient and reestablished capital Jerusalem, as well as in its biblical heartland – the regions of Judea and Samaria – mistakenly known to most of the world by the fictional term, the West Bank. This position is taken by leading candidate Hillary Clinton, who infamously phoned Prime Minister Benjamin Netanyahu during her term as Secretary of State to sternly lecture him for 45 minutes about the illegality of Israel granting a building permit to Jews in Israel's capital city. Her views have not changed.

Perhaps it's time for Jews and other supporters of Israel to take a closer look at the Republicans? Most of the GOP candidates were vehemently opposed to the Iran nuclear deal, and they also tend to support giving Israel a free hand in crushing the terrorism, although some are vague on specifics when it comes to the Palestinian state issue. Let's examine those who are leading in the polls:

Donald Trump –

Trump's statements about how he loves Israel, and how bad a deal the Iran nuclear deal is, as well as his calls for a very strong American policy against ISIS – all of these are certainly positive, although Mr. Trump has so far been very short on specifics about the Palestinian state issue. His daughter Ivanka is a convert to Judaism and she and her Jewish husband and children are reported to be Sabbath-observant members of an Orthodox synagogue. While that may have a positive influence on Trump's Land of Israel views, the jury is out until we hear specifics.

Ben Carson –

Dr. Carson is on record as opposing the "land for peace" formula of Israel surrendering land in exchange for a peace treaty. In March of 2015, he responded to a questioner, saying, "We need to look at fresh ideas. I don't have any problem with the Palestinians having a state, but does it need to be within the confines of Israeli territory?" His views tend to be historically/biblically based, which emphasizes that they are genuine and not just produced for political consumption. Carson has also expressed deep concern and has been very vocal about the Islamic Jihadist threat to Western civilization. Such an understanding inherently makes him sympathetic to Israel's challenges as the one bastion of freedom in the hostile Islamic Middle East.

Ted Cruz –

Senator Cruz has spoken out consistently about the importance of letting Israel decide for itself on issues of war and peace and on the Palestinian state issue. He has stated clearly that settlement is an internal Israeli issue that the United States administration should not be involved in. Says Cruz, "I don't believe an American president should be dictating to the nation of Israel where Israelis can choose to live. And the fact that Israelis choose to live in Judea and Samaria is not justification for terrorism or murder." It's also relevant to note that Cruz used the correct historical, biblical terms for the so-called West Bank, making him unique among most of the leading candidates.

Marco Rubio –

Rubio has said that if elected, he would not honor the Iran nuclear deal and has also called for the United States to stand with Israel "unconditionally" in its battle against its enemies. While strongly blaming the Palestinian Authority (PA) for the current terrorism and the tensions between Israel and the PA, Senator Rubio has referred to the two state solution, which generally means the "land for peace" formula as the desired goal. He has qualified that by emphasizing that it's not a realistic goal at this time. According to Rubio, "That's the ideal outcome, but the conditions for a two-state solution at this moment do not exist." This places him firmly in the camp of Prime Minister Netanyahu, who has repeatedly expressed support for a demilitarized Palestinian state in Judea and Samaria, as long as it recognizes Israel as a Jewish state.

◆◆◆

The GOP candidates cited above are clearly sympathetic

towards Israel, certainly far more than Clinton or Sanders. The problem is that it requires great courage for the candidates to be more Jewish than Israel's political "Pope," otherwise known as Benjamin Netanyahu, who sorry to say, has been weak, both on fighting terrorism and on asserting Israel's right to its Land. Nonetheless, the difficult question should be asked of the GOP candidates, "If the PA publicly recognizes Israel as a Jewish state and agrees not to have heavy weapons, would he support the establishment of such an Islamic terrorist nation in Israel's biblical heartland, in the strategically-vital hills overlooking Ben Gurion International Airport?"

Shouldn't that question be asked of Netanyahu, as well?

Where is Bennett's Voice?

"To sin by silence, when we should protest, makes cowards out of men."

(Ella Wheeler Wilcox, American writer)

Jewish Home party leader Naftali Bennett has been very quiet these days, as has his sidekick, Justice Minister Ayelet Shaked. As the terrorism rages and the unofficial, yet obvious building permit freeze in the biblical heartland of Judea and Samaria continues to be enforced by Israel's political leadership, why is Bennett silent?

There is a background to this. When the current Islamic terror wave of shootings, stabbings, firebombs, and rocks began, Minister Bennett went on a fact-finding tour of Jerusalem and then shared his reaction with the public, "I just came back from the field. I questioned soldiers and policemen," said Bennett, "and they told me that they are not responding to provocations. I visited the Old City, and the police officers stationed there told me that there was no deterrence and that no one was afraid of them. Enough restraint on our part! Enough being so worried! We must act with force and determination."

Prime Minister Netanyahu was enraged, venting at the subsequent Cabinet meeting that no minister in his Cabinet will voice opposition to the government position (meaning his weak-kneed, defensive position), while at the same time remaining a minister in his government. Bennett was apparently intimidated by this not so veiled threat. I say "apparently," because he hasn't expressed this publicly, but his silence since that October 5th Cabinet meeting speaks volumes. The deafening silence wasn't even broken after the supposedly "pro-settlement" Netanyahu boasted recently that in his recent years in office, he has enabled less building starts in Judea and Samaria than any of the previous prime ministers.

Why is Naftali Bennett sitting quietly in the coalition, as the government takes no visible offensive action to stop the terrorism that is plaguing our nation every day? Why is the leader of the Jewish Home, as well as his fellow minister Shaked, remaining silent, as the Jewish communities of Judea and Samaria, his main power base, are being suffocated by the planned and actual scarcity of housing? When other parties in the coalition are upset about certain Netanyahu actions, or even just his statements, they don't hesitate to voice those objections loud and clear, including implied threats of impending havoc within the coalition if demands are not met. Then when they speak behind closed doors afterwards, Netanyahu listens.

There has been one recent exception to Bennett's silence policy. Last week, he called on protesters to accept the Supreme Court order to destroy a Givat Ze'ev synagogue, based on the usual dubious Arab land claims, which in turn are usually based on illegal land grants from the 1948-67 Jordanian occupation of Judea and Samaria. Furthermore, when has the Supreme Court ordered the destruction of the many illegally built mosques, where calls to violence against Jews are proclaimed every day? When will Bennett voice his firm objection to that?

The ostensible political leader of Religious Zionism must be the voice of Jewish pride, not retreat, of strength, not weakness, of faith, not fear. The silence must end.

Trudeau's Islamic Tsunami on the Way?

"The process of (Islamic) settlement is a "Civilization-
Jihadist Process"… The Ikhwan (Arabic for brothers)
must understand that their work in America is a kind
of grand Jihad to eliminate and destroy the Western
civilization from within, and sabotage its miserable
house by their hands and the hands of the believers…"

(Muslim Brotherhood document, discovered by the American FBI)

C anadian Prime Minister Justin Trudeau, after
less than a month in office, is hastily living up
to his reputation as the northern Obama. His
announcement that he is determined to keep his campaign
pledge to welcome in at least 25,000 Syrian immigrants is
raising many eyebrows, as the terrorist threat from such
newcomers becomes more and more apparent with the most
recent Islamic terrorist massacre in France.

President Barack Hussein Obama, who grew up as a
Muslim, has also announced similar intent concerning the
immigration, much to the dismay of some thirty American
governors who have voiced strong opposition. Obama's plan
comes as no surprise, given that he has long been animated
by his desire to make the United States a more Muslim
nation, but what is Trudeau's excuse? Doesn't he see what
is happening across the ocean on the European continent?

The current invasion of Europe by the tsunami of Muslim
immigrants will rapidly hasten the transformation of Europe
from a modern, polite civilization into a third world Islamic
civilization. In the short term, we will see the strengthening of
the right-wing anti-Islamification parties throughout Europe.
The accusations of "Islamophobia" will increase as the very

rational fear of Islam will be called racist by those who wish to see a worldwide Islamic takeover.

Canada and the United States are not far behind, which brings us back to the question of why a leftist like Trudeau would encourage a surge of Islamic immigration. Is it solely a result of the pretentious "caring" of the Left, which supposedly feels the "pain" of these refugees? Well, no, and actually the proverbial cat is crawling out of the bag. For a number of years, there has been a strange collusion between the Left and the Islamic ideologues. Both are trying to transform Western Civilization from a primarily Judeo-Christian one into a society of their respective choosing. The Muslims want to create an Islamic Caliphate, in which Islam would rule all. The secular Left wants to create a sort of nouveau Pagan, hedonistic society in which same-sex marriage, abortion on a whim, and fanatic animal rights would be the norm. This worldview would seem to be at odds with that of the Muslims, but it is the hatred of Judeo-Christian civilization, and also of Israel that binds them together.

Ultimately, the secular Left would suffer severe oppression from the Islamic Caliphate, of an intensity that would destroy their lives. Persecution of homosexuals, of women, and sexual abuse of children would quickly become the norm. But since most secularists believe in living for today, why worry about it now?

Bennett Now Calling for Stronger Action: "Irresponsible?"

"It is no use saying, 'We are doing our best.' You have got to succeed in doing what is necessary."

(Winston Churchill, British statesman)

I wrote an article recently, calling on Minister Naftali Bennett to end his disturbing silence about the horrific security situation in Israel, As one who knows that stronger actions are needed to stop the terror wave, I was troubled by his silence. Just nine days later, I am happy to see that Bennett is speaking out again, advocating for a strong, offensive military operation similar to Israel's Operation Defensive Shield in 2002.

Not surprisingly, the political cowards in the defense establishment are already launching vicious personal attacks against Bennett, calling him "a messiah claimant" and "an inciter," adding that Bennett's criticism is "irresponsible."

The reality is that Mr. Bennett's demand for stronger offensive measures was very reasonable, a fulfillment of his responsibility as a public servant. His job is to boldly raise important issues for national discussion.

Blatantly out of bounds were the snide, hateful personal attacks on Bennett, a member of the Security Cabinet. Using a pejorative such as "messiah claimant" is a poorly-veiled attempt to avoid responding to the security challenges faced by ordinary Israelis, by crudely implying that a religious Israeli cannot rationally analyze the situation.

The truth is quite the opposite. It is the anonymous defense officials who are irresponsible, and they should be firmly put in their places, by their boss, Defense Minister

Moshe Ya'alon. Perhaps then, they can put their focus where it belongs, on providing security for Israel's citizens. As for Ya'alon, it would be prudent for him to read up on Operation Defensive Shield, which was a comprehensive assault on the Islamic terrorist organizations throughout Judea and Samaria. Thousands of weapons were seized and hundreds of terrorists were eliminated, thereby preventing many future attacks. Furthermore, vast quantities of documents were seized from the Mukata, the Palestinian Authority headquarters in Ramallah, thereby proving its complicity in financing and inciting the terror war on Israel.

Despite the feeble claims by the defense establishment, the circumstances now are not so different than what was in 2002. Unless the defense officials quoted above are living in a bubble, or perhaps in some fantasy play land, they must have noticed that in the past two months, there have been daily, and often hourly terrorist attacks on Jewish Israelis of all ages, ethnic groups, and religious persuasions. These attacks, most likely orchestrated from above, have been on a scale that has not been seen since the horrible period of 2000-2005. The tentative, defensive steps taken to date are obviously not enough, and the time has come to examine and implement serious offensive measures that will put an end to the terror wave once and for all. A full-scale military operation in Ramallah, Shechem, and Hebron, including a massive assault on the entire Palestinian Authority infrastructure would be a very good start.

Military Idiots

"We have heard of the pride of Moab – he is exceedingly proud – of his haughtiness, his pride, his arrogance and his self-exaltation."

(Jeremiah 48:29-30)

Mediocre generals, and even great generals, do not necessarily make wise politicians. While many of the top officers in the Israel Defense Forces (IDF) have for years used the military as a launching pad into the world of political leadership, they often expose their lack of humility by trying to influence political policy while still in uniform. Even worse, they often reveal their gross ignorance, by recommending excessive reliance on diplomacy in the face of terror.

According to a report today in Ynet news service, the Central Command of the IDF is proposing to give more weapons to Palestinian Authority (PA) security forces in order to "ease conditions" for the so-called Palestinians. Such proposals would be laughable if they weren't so incredibly dangerous. For over two months, ordinary Israelis have been suffering from a continuing onslaught of terrorist attacks. These assaults have been carried out in all parts of the country, but recently with a particular focus on Jerusalem, Judea, and Samaria. The victims of these brutal stabbings, shootings, car attacks, and firebombs have been Jews and every single attack has been intended to kill Jews, not Arabs, and therefore, the obvious questions must be asked:

What in the world is going through the minds of the military leadership that they are looking to "ease conditions" for the "Palestinians?" And to do so by giving them more weapons? Who is under attack here, the Muslims or the Jews? Minister Yisrael Katz was correct when he rightly pointed out yesterday that the Palestinian terror war is not an intifada, or rebellion. It is, in fact, the front lines of a Jihadist war against all non-Muslims and specifically the Jews, who are referred to as pigs and monkeys in the classic Islamic sources.

Israel should be using its very capable military forces to seize all weapons from the PA-controlled areas and to expel those who are giving the orders to kill us. Giving weapons to the PA, to those who have been financing and glorifying Islamic terrorism against Israelis for the past twenty-five years is absolutely irresponsible, and even insane.

It could be that the IDF generals who made those recommendations to the government are aiming to launch their eventual political careers with the latest reincarnation of the left-wing Labor party or the far-left Meretz. If so, they can rightly be accused of reckless political corruption, endangering the lives of their fellow Israeli citizens for their own political gain. If not, a good psychological evaluation is badly needed. Suicidal tendencies have no place in the IDF and certainly not in its leadership.

Banning Muslim Immigration: Is Trump Right?

"Islam isn't in America to be equal to any faith, but to become dominant. The Koran should be the highest authority in America, and Islam the only accepted religion on Earth."

(Omar Ahmed, Chairman of CAIR:
The Council on American-Islamic Relations)

Republican candidate Donald Trump is controversial. He says a lot of things that upset a lot of people. Recently, he has made a few statements that show his lack of experience on issues that concern Israel. Hopefully, he will find the humility to learn and evolve on those issues, but on the challenge of Muslim immigration to America, he is right on target.

The North American continent is now seeing the same trends of Muslim immigration and increasing Islamic terrorism that its European counterpart has been experiencing for years. The demographic threat isn't as obvious as in Europe, where large and hostile Muslim populations in major cities along with growing Jihadist agitation have been increasingly serious challenges for some years now. The writing is on the wall for America, as well. As Muslim immigration continues and the Muslim birthrate remains high, the terrorist threats increase, as do the calls for Sharia, the oppressive Islamic legal system that bans non-Islamic religious expression, and allows wife beating, polygamy, and forms of child abuse. Alongside the very high Muslim birthrate in the United States, the non-Muslim American birthrate remains very low, as delayed marriage, same-sex marriage, and a creeping anti-traditional family culture takes root.

Do your basic arithmetic and see where it's going. The attacks on the World Trade Center in New York, the Ft. Hood attack, the Boston bombing, and the San Bernardino attack are only the tip of the iceberg, or as I call it, the "Islamic Tsunami," that is rapidly making its way to American cities and towns across the land.

That is, if nothing is done to stop it. And that is where candidate Trump is tapping into some very real concerns that many Americans are correctly feeling. No, this is not Islamophobia, some falsely defined irrational fear, or anxiety of a non-existent threat. It is, in fact, a very real fear of a very real threat, so why is it so hard for so many Americans to accept a policy of banning Muslim immigration? Even if craftily defined as a ban on immigration by those who have spent significant time in Muslim-dominated countries, and/or who have had any ties with terrorist groups, why do Americans have such a difficult time accepting restrictions on the immigration of Muslims?

The United States was established on the basis of religious freedom. The Founders left the establishment religious tyranny behind and created American freedom for all, and for that reason, Americans find it distasteful to limit the freedom of any religion. But Islam is not just another religion, with a tiny "fringe" group called "Radical Islam." If that were the case, the free world wouldn't be under attack by a long list of Islamic terrorist armies around the world. The very core of Islam is based on Jihad, which means holy war against what the Koran calls the unbelievers, specifically non-Muslims. Such a philosophy of intolerance is anti-American and anti-freedom, and if allowed to grow in the United States, it poses a serious threat to the very religious freedoms that Americans hold so dear.

And that is why banning Muslim immigration to the United States is morally sound policy. Yes, full freedom is a noble ideal, but no free country has an obligation to self-destruct. To grant freedom to those who would use that freedom to undo the freedom of others makes no sense.

Pledging Allegiance to Jihad in the USA

"Those who stand for nothing, fall for anything."

(Alexander Hamilton, one of the founders
of the United States of America)

As reported on Fox News, a Muslim Civil Court judge was sworn in this week in New York City using the Koran, the holy book of Islam, as a testament to her radical Islamic belief system.

In the realm of "political correctness," the Left's nihilistic value system, Islamic values are okay, not just in the legal system, but in politics as well. According to the Left, the Bible should no longer be the basis of society's civil principles, but a judge or a politician can now be sworn in on the Koran, a book that calls repeatedly for Jihad – holy war against all non-Muslims. That same judge or politician can now legally swear allegiance to the Islamic ideology that allows wife-beating, abuse of children, and other crimes that would usually be considered aberrations in Western countries.

Many extreme liberal pundits say that there is nothing problematic in this. They insist that it's just an isolated case of granting equal religious rights to a religious minority. However, such claims are fallacious at best. The sad reality is that the West is being threatened by a dangerous ideology. A society that pledges allegiance to the biblical principle of "Love your neighbor as yourself" cannot live at peace with a society within that calls for Jihad.

"The fundamental basis of this nation's laws was given to Moses on the Mount (Sinai)."

(Harry S. Truman, February 15, 1950)

A lot has changed since the days of President Truman when the Judeo-Christian roots of the American nation were still well understood. In recent years, the Islamic attempts to gain influence in the American political system have been focused not just on the legal system, but on supporting candidates who are supportive of Islam, mainly in the Democratic Party. Several individual politicians have been seeking to work their way through the system, exploiting democracy to advance the tyranny of Islam. One such individual is Democratic Congressman Keith Ellison, a convert to Islam, who was elected as the first Islamic Congressman from his home state of Minnesota. Ellison was sworn into his new position by then House Speaker Nancy Pelosi. The Washington Post reported (January 3, 2007) that Ellison would be sworn in, not on a Bible, but on a Koran, that had been owned once by Thomas Jefferson.

This departure from congressional norms raised many an eyebrow. Ellison claimed that Jefferson appreciated the diversity of America and that the Koran was part of that.

"It demonstrates that from the very beginning of our country, we had people who were visionary, who were religiously tolerant, who believed that knowledge and wisdom could be gleamed from any number of sources, including the Koran," Ellison said in a telephone interview several days before the swearing in.

However, if Jefferson were alive today, he would have told a very different story. Jefferson had bought his Koran in order to learn and understand the Islamic ideology, hence the mentality, of the Barbary Pirates, the Islamic terror group that was harassing American traders at sea. Under the presidencies of George Washington and John Adams, the terrorists had been demanding, as well as receiving, many millions of dollars in protection money from the United States government to allow safe passage for American ships.

Upon taking office, President Jefferson put an end to that cynical game, changing course and thereby saving the nation in its infancy. His knowledge of the Koran, which he had read specifically for this purpose ("Know thine enemy"), gave him the background that confirmed for him the nature of the beast. Lacking a navy, he decided to send the Marines to "the shores of Tripoli" to defeat the Barbary Pirates.

Islam is contrary to the values of the free world. A majority of Americans and Europeans, and even some Israelis seem oblivious to the true Jihadist nature of Islam. Until we educate ourselves about that unpleasant truth and start taking action, the creeping Islamic tsunami will continue to infiltrate the legal and political infrastructure of the United States, as well as the rest of the free world, ultimately destroying it from within.

The Duma Scandal: Innocent Until Proven Guilty?

"Maimonides taught that it is better that ten criminals go free than to let one innocent man be executed."

(Rabbi Norman Lamm, Chancellor of Yeshiva University)

In every country that protects the legal rights of its citizens, the maxim "innocent until proven guilty" is an iron-clad pillar of law and is fiercely protected by political and legal authorities. Therefore, the seeming departure from that norm when it occurs in a country like Israel is particular disturbing.

In July of 2015, there was an arson attack on a home in the Samarian town of Duma, in which an Arab couple and their infant son were killed. After the attack, and despite the fact that no arsonist was found at the scene of the crime, it was quickly announced by the Israeli police and later by Defense Minister Moshe Ya'alon, among others, that Jews were the perpetrators of the crime. Several young Jews were quickly taken into custody without being formally charged. These were followed by others, including minors, again with no formal charge.

After some six months in secret solitary confinement, during which time hardly any visits by legal counsel have been permitted, facts are beginning to emerge, not of any serious evidence pertaining to the crime, evidence which appears to be non-existent, but of horrific acts being carried out by the Israeli Shabak (Internal Security Agency) as part of their investigation of the Duma crime. It now seems increasingly apparent that some of the young men and teenaged boys in custody are being subjected to severe forms of torture, behavior virtually unheard of in a democratic society. One of the minors reportedly has attempted to commit suicide after a particularly vicious torture session. Damning audio evidence has surfaced of the suspect begging for mercy and revealing several torture methods – including being tied upside down till his hands burned, being kept awake all night, and having his back pummeled to the point of needing medical attention.

Attorney Adi Keidar, after finally meeting his young client, revealed that senior investigators often come in and beat him cruelly in sensitive body organs, until at a certain point he doesn't feel anything anymore, including "kicks and slaps."

Keidar also provided testimony regarding another suspect, saying, "he was prevented from sleeping for three days. The investigators started pulling his head back and he threw up violently. After he saw a doctor who said he needs rest, they continued the abuse."

As has been expressed by most Israelis many times since the Duma attack was announced, the culprits, whether they are Jews or Muslims, should be punished severely for the crime in Duma, but it now appears that a different crime is being perpetrated by those who are being entrusted to protect the public from criminals. With no evidence against the young Jews, who have been incarcerated for months with no formal charges in place, it appears that we are witnessing a travesty of justice that is more fitting in the most oppressive of dictatorships.

Would such torture and abuse of the fundamental presumption of innocence be carried out against the many Muslim terrorists who have, amid abundant concrete evidence, been launching daily terror attacks against Israeli citizens? I think not. In fact, it's absolutely obscene to equate the two legal situations, but that is what common sense observers and ordinary citizens are being forced to do.

I call on Prime Minister Benjamin Netanyahu and Defense Minister Ya'alon to prove that we are, indeed, an integral part of the free world, by immediately freeing these young Jewish prisoners for lack of evidence, and then commissioning an independent investigation into the apparently abhorrent conduct of the legal-political authorities in the handling of this case.

The Brazil Issue and Jewish Pride

"Those indoctrinated by leftist thinking become largely incapable of making accurate moral judgments."

(Dennis Prager, radio talk show host, columnist)

The controversy over Dani Dayan's appointment as Israel's Ambassador to Brazil has stirred up a diplomatic row that is an unfortunate test of our pride as a sovereign nation. What has caused this conflict and what can we learn from it?

The Argentinian-born Dayan happens to be a long-time resident of Samaria and the former head of the Yesha Council, an advocacy group for Jewish communities in Judea and Samaria. Despite its approval by the Israeli cabinet, the Dayan appointment has hit into a surprising wall of opposition, all based on his right-of-center views and his place of residence. The Brazilian government, in a rare departure from diplomatic protocol, has held up granting its consent to the appointment for more than four months and is now sending out the message that Israel should choose someone else.

Despite support from leading politicians across the Israeli political spectrum for what is, in fact, a diplomatic, not political appointment, numerous supposedly non-political appointees from past administrations have gotten involved; frantically trying to torpedo what should have been a routine approval process. In an embarrassing display of politically-biased unprofessional behavior, three former Israeli ambassadors, including former Foreign Ministry Director General Alon Liel, have been acting against the will of Israel's elected government, using their influence with the government of Brazil to demand that Brasilia reject Dayan's appointment. This has apparently been done in close coordination with the Palestinian Authority, the same PA that has been inciting and funding a daily terror war against Israel.

"V'Lamalshinim al tehi tikva."
For those who slander there should be no hope.

(From the weekday Amidah prayers)

For years, Israel's right-of-center parties have never gotten in the way of ambassadorial appointees who may have had left-of-center views, and such appointees have been much more common, especially during the Yitzchak Rabin-Shimon Peres-Ehud Barak era. It was always understood, at least publicly, that an Israeli diplomat is simply an advocate for Israel, whatever his place on the political spectrum. The appointment of Dayan, with his pro-settlement views, has changed all that. Suddenly, the diplomatic elites no longer value the principle that we don't let internal politics get in the way of capable, professional diplomacy on behalf of Israel. The stench of political bias coming from the diplomatic Left that is busy scheming with the Palestinian Authority is so obvious and the breach of diplomatic protocol by Brazil is so blatant that the Netanyahu government should be fighting it tooth and nail. If the Brazilian government refuses to accept Israel's appointee, the current Brazilian Ambassador to Israel should be sent home.

It all comes down to a question of Jewish pride, the basic national pride that should be a given for us in situations like this. A country that accepts the non-recognition of its capital, as Israel tacitly does with its general public silence about the issue of Jerusalem, will not be given any respect when it comes to a relatively small issue like diplomatic appointments. A proud nation doesn't fear the ramifications of every diplomatic offensive, but instead takes such action when needed.

The Dayan case calls for such a bold approach, and no compromise.

Ya'alon's Weakness in the Face of Terror

"Fighting terrorism is not unlike fighting a deadly cancer. It can't be treated just where it's visible – every diseased cell in the body must be destroyed."

(David Hackworth, American army officer)

The Defense Minister of the State of Israel should project an image of strength that sends Israel's enemies scrambling for cover. Therefore, it is extremely disturbing to see Defense Minister Moshe Ya'alon's repeated acts of weakness opposite the Islamic terrorist organizations that have been attacking Israeli citizens daily for the past three months.

The latest in a series of pusillanimous maneuvers by Ya'alon is yesterday's handover to the Palestinian Authority (PA) of the bodies of eight terrorists who carried out recent terror attacks in which they were subsequently neutralized by Israel's security forces.

On October 14, the Israeli Cabinet voted to no longer release any dead terrorist bodies, but Ya'alon is blatantly subverting that decision, claiming that his view is more consistent with the worldview that there is no purpose in holding these bodies and that if held, it could provoke unrest in the Palestinian street.

As if there is no unrest now? As if Palestinian "unrest" is a mere part of a spontaneous "year of rage" not directed and financed from the top? Such a ridiculous presumption by Ya'alon – that Israeli actions cause Jihadist terrorism – shows an appalling ignorance unbefitting of Israel's top security official. Ya'alon's limp-wrist policy of giving in to terrorists is in direct defiance of the will of the Israeli people and of common sense. The PA, as always, will happily pocket this latest Israeli concession, as it continues to hold the bodies of Israeli soldiers seized in the last Gaza conflict. The Muslims know weakness when they see it, and they have found that weak link in the more appropriately titled, "Weakness Minister" Moshe Ya'alon, who sadly, has been entrusted with our national defense and is failing miserably in that task. And the terror war on Israel's citizens continues at a pace of their choosing.

Meanwhile, the PA's Chief Murderer Mahmoud Abbas and his henchmen are having a good laugh at our expense in the Mukata, the PA's terror headquarters in Ramallah. What will Ya'alon give them next?

Not Lone Wolves

"Liberty for wolves is death to the lambs."

(Isaiah Berlin, Latvian-British philosopher)

It has been a horrible 24 hours of terrorism in the hills of Judea. Thirty-eight-year-old Dafna Meir was brutally stabbed and murdered at the entrance to her home in Otniel in the presence of her young children. The very next morning, a 30-year-old pregnant woman, Michal Froman, was stabbed repeatedly in the village of Tekoa. She is now fighting for her life in a Jerusalem hospital.

These two attacks have typified the hundreds of attacks that ordinary Israelis have suffered from in recent months. A substantial number of them have been multiple stabbings and most of the recent attacks have been carried out in Judea, in Samaria, or in eastern Jerusalem – in the biblical heartland of Israel. After each attack, Prime Minister Benjamin Netanyahu and other Cabinet members promise to catch the perpetrator. They tell us that it's very difficult to stop "lone wolf" attacks, but that the individual "wolves" will be hunted down.

Promises and all good intentions aside, the concept of lone wolf attacks does not apply to the current situation. The sad fact is that Israel's political leadership should, and probably does know better, but is avoiding stating the truth because of the political implications. While the terror machine has been sure to hit a variety of places in order to spread terror throughout the broader Israeli populace, it's not an accident that most of the recent attacks have been in the biblical heartland. There are no lone wolves. These attacks are being coordinated and financed by the Palestinian Authority

(PA), whose ideological wolves understand that the biblical heartland, where the biblical prophets and judges walked, is Israel's raison d'etre, its basis for the Jewish claim to the Land of Israel. They know that when they attack Judea, Samaria, and Jerusalem, they are putting an Islamic knife in the heart of the people of Israel and the God of Israel in the name of Allah. Isolated "lone wolves" don't plan such a terror wave. Individuals don't stab pregnant women because of "frustration" or imaginary "rage", but they do if they've been led to believe that they will be rewarded financially or sexually for fulfilling the Islamic precept of Jihad, or holy war against non-Muslims. The Palestinian Authority of Mahmoud Abbas and its terrorist organizations, along with the PA's government-controlled media is the real culprit.

Rather than just hunting down the so-called lone wolves with their bloody knives, the main targets should be the official wolves and wild donkeys that sit in Ramallah, Shechem, Hebron, and Gaza – ordering, encouraging, and financing the terrorism. Their headquarters should be attacked mercilessly and leveled to the ground, and their leadership should be deported from the Land of Israel.

The fear of world criticism has crippled Israel's political leaders. They know full well that only such a proactive approach will sharply reduce the attacks, but because of the feared international abuse of Israel, they feel that their hands are tied. Furthermore, some of Israel's leaders claim that anarchy will result from any weakening of the PA.

Every responsible member of the Israeli Cabinet, as a public servant, must answer the following question and then take appropriate action: What are you more concerned about avoiding – anarchy in the PA, critical UN resolutions, or the deaths of many more Israeli civilians?

Postscript

Now well into 2016, we can look at the last few months, and indeed, much of the trends discussed in this book have continued. Some highlights:

Israeli Politics: Defense Minister and former Chief of Staff Moshe Ya'alon's left-wing turn got so bad that he actually supported a very public speech by one of the IDF generals comparing modern Israel to the Nazis. This led to a strong reprimand by Prime Minister Netanyahu, who reminded Ya'alon that the military's job isn't to express leftist (or rightist) political ideology, rather to take orders from the elected civilian leadership. Ya'alon, who had shown only weakness and lack of resolve when confronting Israel's enemies, was eventually removed from his position and replaced by Avigdor Liberman (Israel Beytenu), thereby bolstering the coalition by increasing it to a more solid plurality of 67 out of the 120 Knesset seats.

American Presidential Clarity in 2016: The erratic, but irrepressible Donald Trump, indeed, did get more specific about Israel, publicly supporting Israel's right to allow Jews to build homes in Judea and Samaria. Furthermore, Trump has been consistent in standing by the principle of a temporary ban on Muslim immigration to the United States, although leaving the details to be worked out later. He subsequently clinched the GOP nomination, with his position greatly strengthened opposite the anti-Israel, pro-Muslim immigration stands of his blatantly corrupt Democratic opponent Hillary Clinton.

The Prospect of War and More Terrorism: As the Hezbollah and Hamas terrorist organizations have continued to build military tunnels and increase their missile supply in the North and the South of Israel, the possibility of another war soon to come is rapidly increasing. An emboldened Iran, assisted by major transfers to its coffers resulting from the Iran nuclear deal, will boost its support for its terrorist friends around the world, as well. More attacks like those in Orlando, Tel Aviv, Brussels, Paris, Boston, and San Bernardino can be expected, as the Islamic ideologues become emboldened by the blindness / confusion in the free world. The Islamic terror threat will only get worse.

Therefore, the two central questions must be asked:

- How will the United States, Canada, and Europe relate to the rapidly increasing Islamic demographic and security threats within their borders?

- Will Israel take offensive action to stop the imminent threats to its very existence?

> "The most important point is, in a time of crisis, there is no way out but for the government to be bold and aggressive."
>
> *(Mark Zandi, economist)*

> "When written in Chinese, the word 'crisis' is composed of two characters. One represents danger and the other represents opportunity."
>
> *(John F. Kennedy, American President)*

While some linguists may have disputed Kennedy's analysis of the Chinese language, the message is clear and poignant. The dangers faced by Israel, by Europe, and by

America, as well as by the rest of the free world, are very frightening. Nonetheless, it would be wise to view these crises calmly, as the great Jewish thinkers always have confronted challenges in our tumultuous history. These crises have often appeared to be intractable problems, but are actually great challenges, wonderful opportunities to do *Tikun Olam*, to create a better world. With abundant courage and determination, and with the help of the Almighty, we will succeed!

About The Author

Davia Rubin is a former mayor of Shiloh, Israel – in the region of Samaria, which together with Judea, is known to much of the world as the West Bank. He is the founder and president of Shiloh Israel Children's Fund (SICF) – dedicated to healing the trauma of children who have been victims of terrorist attacks, as well as rebuilding the biblical heartland of Israel through the children.

SICF was established after Rubin and his three-year-old son were wounded in a vicious terrorist attack while driving home from Jerusalem. Rubin vowed to retaliate – not with hatred, nor with anger, but with compassion – in order to affect positive change for Israel and its children.

Rubin's first book, "God, Israel, & Shiloh: Returning to the Land", tells the story of the very human struggles and triumphs of Israel's complex history, dating back to slavery in Egypt and continuing up to the present. Rubin describes Israel's miraculous return to its biblical heartland, and the subsequent challenge of its residents to rebuild, despite the constant threat of terrorism and the trauma of the many terrorist attacks that have affected their communities.

Rubin's second book, the shockingly prophetic, "The Islamic Tsunami: Israel and America in the Age of Obama", boldly exposes the danger to Israel, America, and Judeo-Christian civilization posed by the Islamic ideologues and their odd collusion with the nihilistic secular Left.

Rubin's third book, "Peace For Peace: Israel in the New Middle East", scans the history of the peace process and explains not just why it hasn't worked, but how it can possibly succeed – by being consistent with biblical principles, historical precedent, and common sense.

Rubin's "Sparks From Zion" shares his sharp analysis of the news from Israel and the Middle East that most of the mainstream media won't tell you, This includes his powerful commentary on the indecisive Israeli response to the Hamas missiles that had prompted the latest war in Gaza.

All of these books are as relevant today as when they were first published.

David Rubin is a very popular blogger on Arutz Sheva, otherwise known as www.IsraelNationalNews.com and his articles have appeared in numerous other publications. A featured speaker throughout North America, Europe, and Israel, David Rubin frequently appears as a guest commentator on Fox News, Newsmax, and other television and radio programs.

Born and raised in Brooklyn, New York, Rubin resides in Israel with his wife and children on a hilltop overlooking the site of Ancient Shiloh. This is the hallowed ground where the Tabernacle of Israel stood for 369 years in the time of Joshua, Hannah, and Samuel the Prophet.

Other Books By David Rubin

Available online at www.DavidRubinIsrael.com/books/
~ Phone orders 1-800-431-1579 ~ Or at a bookstore near you!

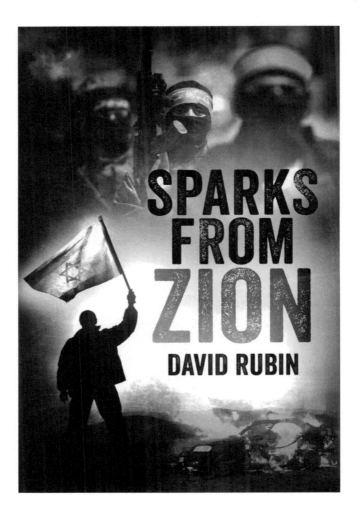

Sparks From Zion
ISBN: 978-0-9829067-6-7

Available online at www.DavidRubinIsrael.com/books/
~ Phone orders 1-800-431-1579 ~ Or at a bookstore near you!

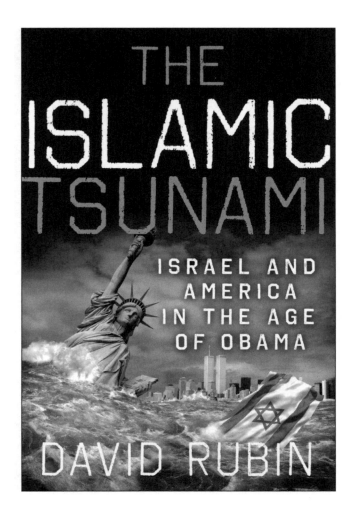

The Islamic Tsunami
Israel And America In The Age Of Obama
ISBN: 978-0-9829067-0-5

Available online at www.DavidRubinIsrael.com/books/
~ Phone orders 1-800-431-1579 ~ Or at a bookstore near you!

Peace For Peace
Israel In The New Middle East
ISBN: 978-0-9829067-4-3

Available online at www.DavidRubinIsrael.com/books/
~ Phone orders 1-800-431-1579 ~ Or at a bookstore near you!

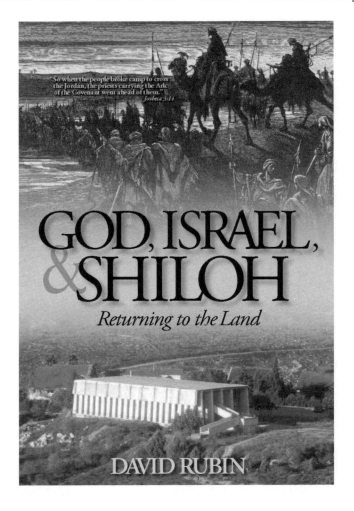

God, Israel, & Shiloh
Returning To The Land
ISBN: 978-0-9829067-2-9